MAKERIFIC WOWS!

54 SURPRISING BIBLE CRAFTS

for ages 3-7

Group

Loveland, Colorado
group.com

Group resources really work!

This Group resource incorporates our R.E.A.L. approach to ministry. It reinforces a growing friendship with Jesus, encourages long-term learning, and results in life transformation, because it's

Relational
Learner-to-learner interaction enhances learning and builds Christian friendships.

Experiential
What learners experience through discussion and action sticks with them up to 9 times longer than what they simply hear or read.

Applicable
The aim of Christian education is to equip learners to be both hearers and doers of God's Word.

Learner-based
Learners understand and retain more when the learning process takes into consideration how they learn best.

MAKERIFIC WOWS!
54 SURPRISING BIBLE CRAFTS
(for ages 3-7)

Copyright © 2018 Group Publishing, Inc. / 0000 0001 0362 4853

Visit our website: **group.com**

CREDITS
Contributing Authors: Elisa Hansen, Laure Herlinger, Karen Pennington, Kelsey Perry, Ali Thompson
Photographer: Rodney Stewart
Chief Creative Officer: Joani Schultz
Editor: Kelsey Perry
Assistant Editor: Becky Helzer
Art Director: Jeff Storm
Lead Designer: RoseAnne Sather
Cover Designer: Jonny Vignola
Interior Designer: Mollie Bickert

Scripture quotations are taken from the Holy Bible, New Living Translation, copyright © 1996, 2004, 2007, 2013, 2015 by Tyndale House Foundation. Used by permission of Tyndale House Publishers, Inc., Carol Stream, Illinois 60188. All rights reserved.

ISBN: 978-1-4707-5341-2

Printed in the United States of America.

10 9 8 7 6 5 4 3 2 1   27 26 25 24 23 22 21 20 19 18

INTRODUCTION

Supplement your Bible lessons in a fun, hands-on way with 3-D crafts from the popular Dig In curriculum! Lots of kids love crafts, and everyone loves toys and games! Using the ideas in this book, your 3- to 7-year-olds will make crafts that are way more than just another piece of paper to hang on the fridge. Kids will make interactive, usable crafts and toys, including a board game, superhero cape, play cellphone, and more.

Each craft ties to a Bible point focusing on the life of Jesus and uses simple supplies you can find at local retailers...in your supply closet...or even in your trash! The Scripture and topical indexes at the back of the book make it easy to find a craft that goes with your Bible lesson.

Get ready for no more crafts left behind in the classroom or discarded on the floor of the car! These crafts get kids making things they'll want to keep while reinforcing the Bible point in their hearts!

CHECK iT OUT!

Table of Contents

AN ANGEL ANNOUNCES JESUS' BIRTH » Announcing Angels 8-9
(Luke 1:26-38; Matthew 1:18-25)

THE FIRST CHRISTMAS » Bethlehem Barns 10-13
(Luke 2:1-7)

JESUS, THE LIGHT OF THE WORLD, IS BORN » Crafty Candles 14-15
(Luke 2:1-20)

SIMEON AND ANNA SEE JESUS » Lifesaver Gift Bags 16-17
(Luke 2:21-40)

WISE MEN WORSHIP KING JESUS » Starry Crowns................................18-19
(Matthew 2:1-18)

JESUS SPEAKS WITH THE RELIGIOUS TEACHERS » We Ask Jesus Mural........20-21
(Luke 2:41-52)

JOHN BAPTIZES JESUS » Proud Father Paintings 22-25
(Matthew 3; Luke 3:21-22)

SATAN TEMPTS JESUS » The Right Way Spinners 26-31
(Matthew 4:1-11; Mark 1:12-13; Luke 4:1-13)

JESUS CALLS DISCIPLES » Changing Faces................................32-37
(Mark 1:16-20; John 1:35-51)

JESUS PERFORMS HIS FIRST MIRACLE » Color-Imprinted Jars 38-41
(John 2:1-12)

NICODEMUS VISITS JESUS AT NIGHT » Circle Paintings................................42-43
(John 3:1-21)

JESUS IS REJECTED » Puffy Heart Gifts 44-47
(Luke 4:16-30)

JESUS HEALS PEOPLE » Healing Care Packages 48-51
(Luke 4:38-40; 5:12-16)

JESUS FORGIVES A PARALYZED MAN » *Bible Story Set*.....52-53
(Luke 5:17-26)

A MIRACULOUS CATCH OF FISH » *Fish Mobiles*..................................54-57
(Luke 5:1-11)

WISE AND FOOLISH BUILDER » *Trustworthy Houses* 58-59
(Matthew 7:24-27)

JESUS EATS WITH SINNERS AT MATTHEW'S HOUSE » *Friendship Handprint Books*...60-63
(Matthew 9:9-13)

JESUS HEALS A LAME MAN BY A POOL » *Stand Up and Walk!*...............64-67
(John 5:1-18)

A ROMAN OFFICER DEMONSTRATES FAITH » *Roman Officer Helmets* 68-71
(Luke 7:1-10; Matthew 8:5-13)

JESUS EASES JOHN'S DOUBT » *Superhero Capes*................................72-73
(Matthew 11:1-6; Luke 7:18-23)

PARABLE OF THE FARMER AND THE SEED » *Sweet Flower Gardens*........74-75
(Matthew 13:1-9, 18-23; Luke 8:4-15)

JESUS DESCRIBES HIS TRUE FAMILY » *Family Photo Frames*.....................76-77
(Matthew 12:46-50; Mark 3:31-35; Luke 8:19-21)

JESUS CALMS THE STORM » *Power Over the Windsock* 78-79
(Matthew 8:23-27; Mark 4:35-41; Luke 8:22-25)

JESUS HEALS A BLEEDING WOMAN AND RESTORES A GIRL TO LIFE » *First-Aid Kits*...80-83
(Mark 5:21-43; Matthew 9:18-26; Luke 8:40-56)

JESUS WALKS ON WATER » *Jesus and Peter Walk on Water*.................84-87
(Matthew 14:22-33; Mark 6:45-52; John 6:16-21)

JESUS IS TRANSFIGURED » *Bright as Light*.......................................88-91
(Matthew 17:1-13; Mark 9:2-13; Luke 9:28-36)

PARABLE OF THE GOOD SAMARITAN » *Share Bears* 92-95
(Luke 10:25-37)

Continued ⟶

Table of Contents (continued)

JESUS FEEDS FIVE THOUSAND » Surprise Boxes..................................96-97
(Matthew 14:13-21; Mark 6:30-44; Luke 9:10-17; John 6:1-15)

DISCIPLES ARGUE ABOUT WHO WILL BE THE GREATEST » Thank-You Trophies.......98-101
(Matthew 18:1-6; Mark 9:33-37; Luke 9:46-48)

JESUS FORGIVES A WOMAN » Dry-Erase Boards 102-105
(John 8:1-11)

JESUS VISITS MARY AND MARTHA » Chat Mats 106-107
(Luke 10:38-42)

JESUS HEALS A CRIPPLED WOMAN » Felt-People Marionettes 108-111
(Luke 13:10-17)

JESUS HEALS A BLIND MAN » Blind-to-See Sunglasses.......................112-115
(John 9:1-41)

JESUS CLAIMS TO BE GOD'S SON » Megaphone Hats 116-117
(John 10:22-42)

PARABLES OF THE LOST SHEEP AND LOST COIN » Lost Coin & Sheep Game Boards 118-121
(Luke 15:1-10)

PARABLE OF THE PRODIGAL SON » Piggy Heart Banks 122-125
(Luke 15:11-32)

JESUS RAISES LAZARUS FROM THE DEAD » Wrapped Lazarus 126-129
(John 11:1-44)

JESUS HEALS TEN MEN OF LEPROSY » Thankfulness Tambourines 130-131
(Luke 17:11-19)

JESUS BLESSES THE CHILDREN » Nylon Baby Dolls............................132-133
(Matthew 19:13-15; Mark 10:13-16; Luke 18:15-17)

JESUS HEALS BLIND MEN » "Call on Jesus" Cellphones 134-135
(Matthew 20:29-34; Mark 10:46-52; Luke 18:35-43)

JESUS MEETS ZACCHAEUS » Prayer Pals 136-139
(Luke 19:1-10)

JESUS' TRIUMPHANT ENTRY » Bowl & Cup Donkeys............140-143
(Matthew 21:1-11; Mark 11:1-11; Luke 19:28-40; John 12:12-16)

THE POOR WIDOW'S OFFERING » Coin Wristbands.................144-145
(Mark 12:41-44; Luke 21:1-4)

THE PLOT TO KILL JESUS » He's Sad With Us.........................146-149
(Luke 22:1-6; Matthew 26:1-5, 14-16; Mark 14:1-2, 10-11)

JESUS WASHES HIS DISCIPLES' FEET » Serving Aprons...............150-151
(John 13:1-17)

JESUS IS BETRAYED AND ARRESTED » Heart Binoculars.............152-153
(Matthew 26:47-56; Mark 14:43-52; Luke 22:47-53; John 18:1-11)

JESUS IS PUT ON TRIAL » Bandage Balls..............................154-155
(Matthew 27:15-31; Mark 15:6-15; Luke 23:1-25; John 18:28–19:16)

JESUS IS CRUCIFIED » Stained-Glass Windows............156-159
(Matthew 27:32-61; Mark 15:21-47; Luke 23:26-56; John 19:17-42)

JESUS RISES FROM THE DEAD » Angel Megaphones......160-161
(Matthew 28:1-10; Mark 16:1-11; Luke 24:1-12; John 20:1-18)

THE EMPTY TOMB » Jesus' Tomb.................................162-165
(Luke 23:26–24:12)

THE ROAD TO EMMAUS » Jesus & Friends Finger Puppets.....................166-167
(Luke 24:13-35)

JESUS APPEARS TO DISCIPLES » Jesus Pop-Up Cards......................168-171
(Mark 16:14; Luke 24:36-43; John 20:19-31)

JESUS TALKS WITH PETER » Heart Lacing..............................172-175
(John 13:31-38; 18:15-18, 25-27; 21:15-25)

THE GREAT COMMISSION » Shadow Puppets.........................176-179
(Matthew 28:16-20; Mark 16:15-20; Luke 24:44-53; Acts 1:6-11)

SCRIPTURE INDEX...180-181

TOPICAL INDEX..182-183

AN ANGEL ANNOUNCES JESUS' BIRTH

Luke 1:26-38; Matthew 1:18-25

Supplies

- construction paper (white and beige)
- markers
- glue sticks
- gold or silver chenille wires
- transparent tape

Easy Prep

- Use ½ sheet of white construction paper and tape to make a 4-inch-tall tube for each child.
- Cut a 2-inch circle from beige construction paper for each child.
- Cut two 5-inch-tall hearts out of white paper for each child.
- Cut a 6-inch piece of chenille wire for each child.
- Make a sample craft to show kids.

ANNOUNCING ANGELS

What Kids Will Do

Kids make paper angels with heart wings.

Talk About Angels

Ask:

- **How do we get good news today?**
- **What would be some fun and crazy ways to send a good message?**

Share your own wild idea, such as sending a message by parakeet or spelling it out in cotton candy clouds. Then let children share creative ways they might send a message.

Say: **God sent an angel to give Mary surprising news. It may seem impossible that an angel would talk to a person, but <u>God does the impossible</u>. The angel said that Jesus would be born.**

Show children the sample craft.

Say: **Let's make this angel to remember that <u>God does the impossible</u>.**

Make Angels

Give each child a paper tube, two hearts, a circle, and a 6-inch chenille wire.

Instruct kids to draw an angel face on the circle.

Help them wrap the end of the wire into a loop to make a halo.

Help children glue the heart "wings" to one side of the tube and then glue the face to the other side.

Help kids tape the halos in place.

Children can use their angels to practice saying the Bible point or retelling the story of the angel giving Mary surprising news.

God does the impossible.

THE FIRST CHRISTMAS

Luke 2:1-7

Supplies

- paper plates (1 per child)
- stapler
- scissors
- markers
- wooden ice cream spoons (1 per child)
- craft sticks (2 per child)
- smiley-face stickers (3 per child)
- chenille wires (4 per child)
- cotton balls (1 per child)
- tape
- other stickers
- 1-inch and 2-inch pieces of yarn
- facial tissues (1 per child)

Easy Prep

- Make a sample craft to show kids.

BETHLEHEM BARNS

What Kids Will Do

Kids make scenes for Jesus' birth.

Make the Barn

Say: **Mary and Joseph took a trip to a place called Bethlehem. When they got there, they couldn't find a place to stay, so they stayed in a place like a barn where animals like cows, sheep, and chicken sleep.** Have kids make barn animal sounds.

Say: **While they were in Bethlehem, Mary had her baby. She had baby <u>Jesus—the best gift ever</u>! Let's make something to tell others about how Jesus was born.**

Give each child a paper plate. Explain that a barn is made of wood from a tree. Have children color both sides of their paper plates brown. Encourage them to color both sides completely. As they work, cut each child's plate into four sections like a pie—but don't cut all the way to the center; you want the four parts to remain intact. Just cut about two-thirds of the way to the center for each cut. You can do this before children finish coloring.

As each child finishes coloring, overlap one section of the paper plate (about an inch) with the section to the left of it. Staple those two sections together. Work your way around the plate, overlapping each section with the section to the left of it like a windmill or fan, until all four sections are overlapped and it makes a basket (barn).

Let kids put stickers on their barns while they wait to move on to the next step. As children work, have them talk about something they know about when they were born or babies they know who were born recently. It's okay if all the kids don't have an example; the idea is to get them talking about new babies.

Have kids lay the barns on their sides, and say: **This is like the barn where Mary, Joseph, and baby Jesus stayed. Let's fill it with some of the things from the Bible story.** Remind children that there were probably animals there, too, since animals live in a barn. Give each child a cotton ball, and let kids choose what kind of animal they want it to be.

Make Mary and Joseph

Say: **Mary and Joseph were at the barn before Jesus was born, so let's make Mary and Joseph first.** Give each child two craft sticks. Help children do the following things to make Mary and Joseph:

- Put a smiley-face sticker on the end of each craft stick to be faces for Mary and Joseph.
- Color the craft sticks to give them clothes.
- Wrap chenille wire around the craft sticks in the middle and at the opposite end of the face to make arms and legs.
- Tape yarn pieces to the head end of the craft sticks for hair. (Younger children could use extra help with this step—lay a piece of tape sticky-side up in front of a child, and have him or her place a few pieces of yarn in the center of the sticky side. Then you'll tape the hair in place.)

As children work, remind them that Mary and Joseph were Jesus' parents, and invite them to tell some things about their parents or guardians.

Make Jesus

Say: **Now let's make <u>the best gift ever—baby Jesus</u>.** Give each child a wooden ice cream spoon. Help kids do the following things to make Jesus:

- Put a smiley-face sticker on the end of the spoon for Jesus' face.
- Wrap the spoons in facial tissues like Mary wrapped baby Jesus in cloth. Kids can use tape to secure the tissues.

As kids work, help them talk about things that are special about Jesus or things they love about him.

Retell About Jesus' Birth

Show children how to use the barn and the Mary, Joseph, Jesus, and animal figures to retell the basic story of Jesus' birth, as time allows. Here are some details to include:

- **Mary and Joseph took a long trip to Bethlehem.** (Make Mary and Joseph "walk a long way.")
- **They couldn't find a place to stay.** (Make Mary and Joseph "knock on some doors.")
- **They found a barn where they could stay.** (Make Mary and Joseph go in the barn. Play with the cotton-ball animal.)
- **Mary had baby Jesus.** (Show baby Jesus. Undo and redo his tissue.)
- **Jesus was the best gift ever for Mary and Joseph, and for us.**

Teach children this song to the tune of "I'm a Little Teapot." (Kids can dance their figures around in the barn as they sing the song.)

God gave Jesus to us
as a gift.
He is a good gift;
He is the best!
Jesus is the best gift
of all time.
Thank you, God, for Jesus' love.

Repeat the retelling as time allows.

Say: <u>**Jesus is the best gift ever!**</u> **And you can use your barn to tell everyone all about that!**

JESUS, THE LIGHT OF THE WORLD, IS BORN

Luke 2:1-20

Supplies

- markers
- craft sticks (1 per child)
- orange, yellow, and red tissue paper
- glue sticks
- shakers of glitter
- crayons
- plastic foam cups (1 per child)

Easy Prep

- Cut the tissue paper into easy-to-manage pieces that are approximately 8½x11 inches.
- Make a sample craft to show kids.

CRAFTY CANDLES

What Kids Will Do

Kids make candle sticks.

Make a Light

Say: **Jesus was born to show how much God loves us. Jesus is the light of the world! That means Jesus shines God's love to us. Let's make candles to help us remember that Jesus is the light of the world.**

Have kids color their craft sticks with markers.

As children color, ask:

- **When are you really glad to have a light?**

Have kids tear pieces of orange, yellow, and red tissue paper to make flames. Let children use glue sticks to glue the "flames" to the top of their craft sticks. Let kids glue glitter on the flames, too.

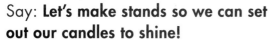

Let It Shine

Say: **The shepherds ran and told everyone the good news that Jesus had been born.**

Ask:

- **Who do you want to tell about Jesus?**
- **What will you tell about Jesus?**

Lead children in singing this song to the tune of "Row, Row, Row Your Boat." Let them wave their "candles" as they celebrate Jesus, the light of the world.

♪ **Shine, shine, shine it bright.
Jesus is the light!
Showing love from God above,
Jesus is the light!**

Say: **Let's make stands so we can set out our candles to shine!**

Have kids use crayons to decorate foam cups and then turn the cups upside down and stick their "candles" in the bottoms of the cups.

Say: **When you go home, you can use your candle and this song to share the good news that Jesus is the light of the world!**

SIMEON AND ANNA SEE JESUS

Luke 2:21-40

Supplies

- sealed envelopes (1 for every 2 children)
- markers
- stickers
- tissue paper
- individually wrapped Life Savers candies (2 per child)
- chenille wires (1 per child)
- hole punch

Easy Prep

- Cut the tissue paper into 4-inch squares.
- Cut the envelopes in half.
- For each envelope half, punch a hole on either side of the opening.
- Make a sample craft to show kids.

LIFESAVER GIFT BAGS

What Kids Will Do
Kids make candy gift bags to give away.

Talk About Gift-Giving
Ask:

- **Who do you love to give gifts to? Why?**

Share your own example first to give children time to think. Then let kids share.

Say: **We give gifts to people we love or people who need something. God wanted to show _us_ how much he loves us, so God gave us a perfect gift. <u>Jesus is God's gift</u>.**

Hold up a Life Savers candy. Explain that this candy is called a Life Saver. Mention that the candy can't _really_ save your life, but it's the same shape as a floating ring that lifeguards use to save people in water.

Say: **In the Bible, a man named Simeon knew that Jesus had come to save people. Jesus is really and truly _our_ life (pause for emphasis) saver because he can save us from the wrong things we do. <u>Jesus is God's gift!</u>**

Jesus is God's gift.

Show children the sample craft.

Say: **You'll get to make a gift bag like this and add a Life Savers candy to it. Then you can give it to someone special and tell that person <u>Jesus is God's gift</u> who came to save us.**

Make the Craft
Hand each child half of an envelope. Let kids use markers and stickers to decorate the envelopes.

Help children loop each end of a chenille wire through the punched holes at the top of their envelopes and then twist the ends to hold the wire in place, creating a handle. Help each child wrap a Life Savers candy in tissue paper and then put it in the gift bag.

Children can stuff another piece of tissue paper on top so it puffs out of the envelope.

Gather children around the gift bags, and pray a blessing over the gifts. Pray for the people who receive these gifts to feel God's mighty love.

Say: **When you give away your gift bag to someone, remember to tell them that <u>Jesus is God's gift</u>, our lifesaver.**

Then give children each a Life Saver candy to enjoy.

WISE MEN WORSHIP KING JESUS

Matthew 2:1-18

Supplies

- crayons
- sheets of white paper
- white butcher paper
- star stickers
- tape

Easy Prep

- Cover sheets of paper with star stickers. Make 1 sheet for every 5 children.
- Cut strips of butcher paper so they're long enough to fit around a child's head (about 18x3 inches). You may want to cut points along one long edge to be the pointed top of a crown.
- Create coloring stations by taping each of the sticker-covered papers to the flat surface of classroom tables and setting out a handful of crayons at each station.
- Make a sample craft to show kids.

STARRY CROWNS

What Kids Will Do
Kids make crayon-rubbing crowns.

Reveal the Stars
Gather children near one of the coloring stations.

Say: **After Jesus was born, wise men traveled to Bethlehem to worship the new king. A bright star showed up in the sky and led them on their trip to see <u>Jesus, the King</u>. In this craft, you'll get to see stars appear, sort of like the wise men did!**

Show kids how to lay a strip of paper over the sticker-covered sheet and then rub a crayon over the paper to see the stars show up.

Give each child a strip of paper, and send children to different coloring stations.

Jesus is the King.

Kids can lay their paper strips over the stickered papers and rub a crayon over the top just as you did. While children are waiting to use the stickered papers, they can color other designs on their paper crowns.

As children finish, wrap each child's crown around his or her head and tape it in place.

Celebrate the King
Say: **Let's celebrate that <u>Jesus is the King</u> by marching and singing.**

Lead children around the room singing this song to the tune of "The Farmer in the Dell."

<u>Jesus is the King!</u>
<u>Jesus is the King!</u>
Let's all go and worship him.
<u>Jesus is the King!</u>

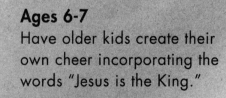

TIP!

Ages 6-7
Have older kids create their own cheer incorporating the words "Jesus is the King."

JESUS SPEAKS WITH THE RELIGIOUS TEACHERS

Luke 2:41-52

Supplies

- bulletin board paper
- sheets of white paper
- crayons
- glue sticks
- markers

Easy Prep

- Cut one 8x4-inch strip of paper per child.
- Write "Jesus is wise" in large letters across the top of the bulletin board paper. You'll want the bulletin board paper to be about 5 feet long for every 20 children. You may want to make several banners if you have a large group.
- Make a sample craft to show kids.

WE ASK JESUS MURAL

What Kids Will Do
Kids make a mural of raised hands.

Ask Questions
Say: **Jesus' parents thought they had lost him. When they looked for him, they found him at the Temple. Jesus was talking to the teachers and asking questions. Asking questions helps us learn. Asking questions helps us be wise like Jesus.**

Sometimes teachers want us to raise our hands when we have a question. Let's make a hand craft with some of our questions.

Raise your hand, and then say: **I have a question: I wonder...** Share about something you wonder about.

Ask:

- **Now it's your turn to ask questions. Raise your hand when you think of a question. What's something you wonder about?**

Choose one child. As he or she shares the question, use a marker to trace the child's hand and part of the arm on a strip of paper. Have all the children repeat that child's question.

Have your teen or adult helpers repeat the same process with the rest of the children in small groups of five or six.

Color "Raised Hands"

Have kids color their "raised hands." As children work, have your helpers write children's questions along the side of the traced arms on children's paper strips.

Create a Mural of "Raised Hands"

As children finish coloring, help them arrange and glue the hands along the bottom of the banner. Place the hands at varying heights all the way across the banner so it looks like a group of raised hands.

Say: **This banner says "Jesus is wise." When we talk to Jesus and ask him questions, we can learn a lot. Jesus can help us be wise. He can help us know what to say and do.**

TIP!

Ages 6-7
Let older kids trace their hands and arms themselves and then each write a question inside the outline.

JOHN BAPTIZES JESUS

Matthew 3; Luke 3:21-22

Supplies

- "Jesus' Baptism" handout (1 copy per child) (p. 25)
- crayons
- blue sidewalk chalk (1 or 2 pieces per child)
- bowls of water
- wet wipes

Easy Prep

- Submerge pieces of blue sidewalk chalk in bowls of water right before you begin the activity. It will take about 5 minutes before kids are able to use them like paint, so the pieces should be ready by the time kids are done coloring.
- Make a sample craft to show kids.

PROUD FATHER PAINTINGS

What Kids Will Do

Kids use water-soaked sidewalk chalk to paint.

Color a Baptism Scene

Say: **Jesus asked John to baptize him. Let's show what Jesus' baptism might've looked like.**

Give everyone a "Jesus' Baptism" handout, and have kids color in John and Jesus with the crayons but leave the water and sky blank.

When the sidewalk chalk is ready, have children use it like finger paint to color in the water and sky. They can rub their fingers on the wet chalk and then transfer it to the paper.

Say: **When John baptized Jesus in the water, the sky opened and the people heard God talk! God said, "Jesus is my dearly loved Son, who brings me great joy." That means <u>Jesus is God's Son</u>, and Jesus makes God happy and proud.**

Jesus is God's Son.

Talk About It

Tell kids a reason your parents are happy with you and proud of you.

Ask:

• **What things make your parents happy or proud?**

Say: **God wanted Jesus to get baptized—and Jesus did! God is proud of Jesus and loves him, just like your parents love you.**

JESUS' BAPTISM

SATAN TEMPTS JESUS

Matthew 4:1-11; Mark 1:12-13; Luke 4:1-13

Supplies

- "Arrow" handout (1 copy for every 4 kids) (p. 29)
- "Spinner" handout (1 two-page handout per child) (p. 30-31)
- crayons
- transparent tape
- clear empty plastic bottles with lids (1 per child)
- several colors of construction paper

Easy Prep

- Remove labels from the bottles.
- Cut apart the sections on the "Arrow" handout, 1 section per child.
- Tear construction paper into small pieces to make "confetti" for younger children to stuff inside the bottles. Older kids can tear the pieces themselves.
- Make a sample craft to show kids.

THE RIGHT WAY SPINNERS

What Kids Will Do

Kids make arrow spinners.

Construct the Spinners

Say: **Jesus shows us the right way. That means he helps us make right choices. Let's make a craft that can help us think about that.**

Give each child a section of the "Arrow" handout, and encourage children to color the arrows. As they finish, help each child tape his or her "Arrow" handout section to a plastic bottle so that the arrows point to the bottle opening.

Next, have kids put construction paper "confetti" in their bottles. It's best to have the kids fill the bottles with anything from just a few pieces of confetti to no more than a quarter full so the confetti can move freely when the bottles spin.

Give each child a two-page "Spinner" handout, and have kids color each section of the spinner with a different color.

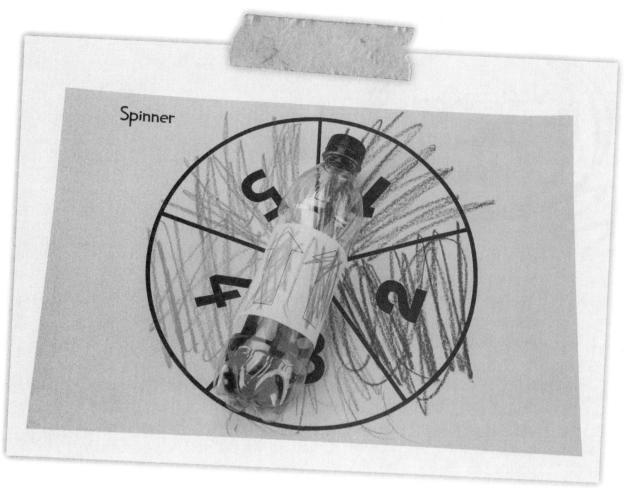

Spinner

As kids work, make a complete spinner for each child by cutting off the edge of one of the handout pages and taping it over the edge of the other handout page.

Play With the Spinners
Say: **Let's play with our spinners. When you spin your bottle on the circle, it points to a number. Let's use that number to help us know how many times to jump.** Demonstrate how to spin one of the bottles, and let children call out the number that the bottle points to when it stops. Have all the kids jump that number of times.

Say: **This time, let's use the spinner to tell us how many times to clap.** Have all the children put their bottles on their circles and spin them.

Point out the number that each child got, and have that child clap that number of times.

Continue having kids choose an action as a group. Then have each child spin his or her own spinner and do the action as many times as the spinner shows. Kids can do actions such as give high-fives, pat others on the back, shake the hands of X number of other kids, stomp their feet, sit down and stand up, close their eyes while they count, or hold hands in groups of X number of kids. For younger children, have the children all spin their bottles at once, but choose only one child's spinner to determine how many times you do something all together as a group.

Jesus shows us the right way.

Say: **In our game, we spun the bottles to see how many times to jump, clap, and many other things. The arrows on the bottle pointed to the right number. Like that, Jesus points the right way. <u>Jesus shows us the right way</u> by what he does and says in the Bible. And we can ask him for help, too.**

Tell kids about a couple of things that Jesus "points to" like an arrow. You can say things like "Jesus points like an arrow to love. Jesus shows us how to love others"; "Jesus points like an arrow to tell the truth. Jesus shows us how to tell the truth"; or "Jesus points like an arrow to sharing. Jesus show us how to share with others."

Invite children to share other good choices that Jesus can show us. Help them say, "Jesus points like an arrow to…"

Say: **Jesus shows us how to make right and good choices. Like our spinning arrows, <u>Jesus shows us the right way</u>.**

TIP!

Ages 6-7
Give older kids a quarter sheet of paper, and have them design and draw several arrows themselves rather than using the "Arrow" handout. They'll want to draw all the arrows facing in one direction, preferably toward a longer side of the quarter sheet of paper.

ARROW

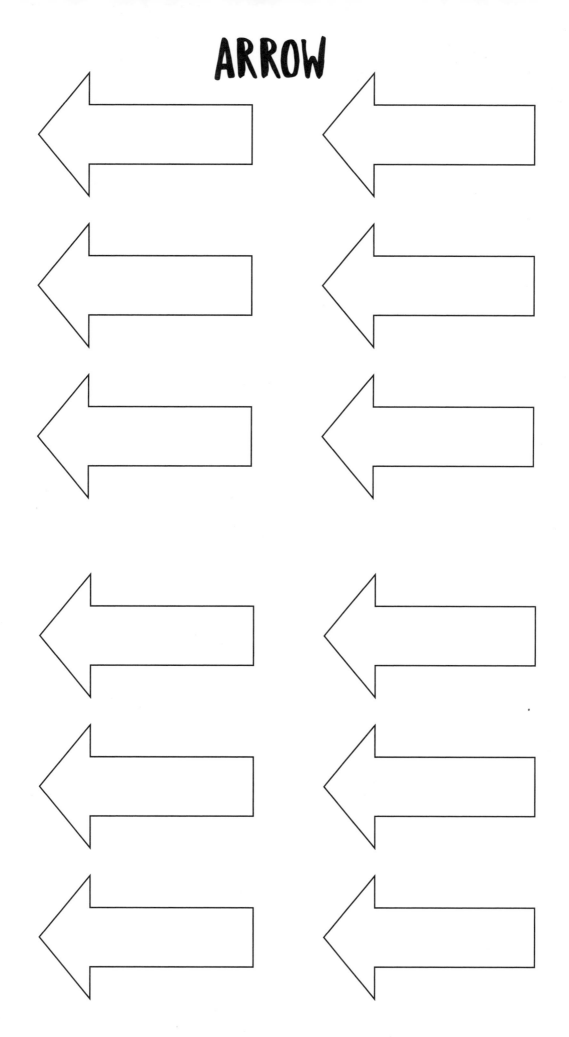

SPINNER

5

4

3

JESUS CALLS DISCIPLES

Mark 1:16-20; John 1:35-51

Supplies

- "Face" handout (1 copy per child) (p. 34)
- "Hat" handout (1 copy per child) (p. 35)
- "Shirt" handout (1 copy per child) (p. 36)
- "Pants" handout (1 copy per child) (p. 37)
- markers
- several colors of yarn
- large resealable plastic bags (1 per child)
- foam stickers (optional)

Easy Prep

- Cut each handout in half.
- Cut at least six 6-inch pieces and six 2-inch pieces of each color of yarn per child.
- Make a sample craft to show kids.

CHANGING FACES

What Kids Will Do

Kids change a character's clothes and face.

Color Each Part

Say: **The Bible tells us how Jesus changed some fishermen's lives. And <u>Jesus can change our lives</u>. Let's make some fun characters that we can change as many times as we want.**

Show children the character set you made. Line up one face, one hat, one shirt, and one set of pants. Show kids how you can change up different pieces by trading out your alternate face, hat, shirt, or pants. Also, switch out the hair. If you have foam stickers, you can use those to make eyes, noses, mouths, ears, or clothing patterns (without actually sticking them on the paper). If you don't have foam stickers, there will just be fewer changes that kids can make.

Have the children color each of their faces, hats, shirts, and pants.

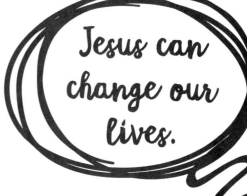

Jesus can change our lives.

Change the Characters

Allow time for children to play with their character sets, changing out the different parts and making different looks.

As kids work, lead them in talking about good changes in their lives, such as going to school, moving to a new home, meeting new friends, or new things they learn that help make their lives better.

Say: <u>**Jesus can change our lives.**</u> **And that's a good thing! When we're friends with Jesus, he makes our every day better!**

Store each child's character set pieces in a large plastic bag so kids can take the sets home without losing any parts.

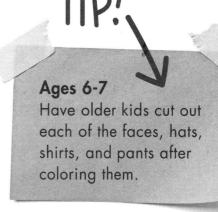

TIP!

Ages 6-7
Have older kids cut out each of the faces, hats, shirts, and pants after coloring them.

FACE

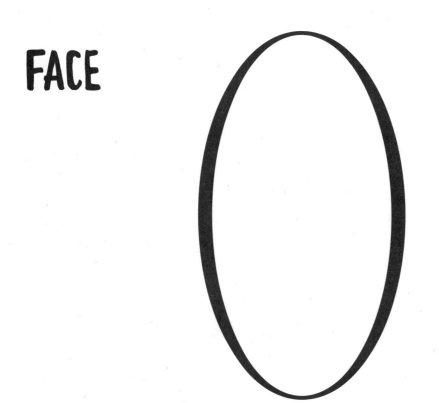

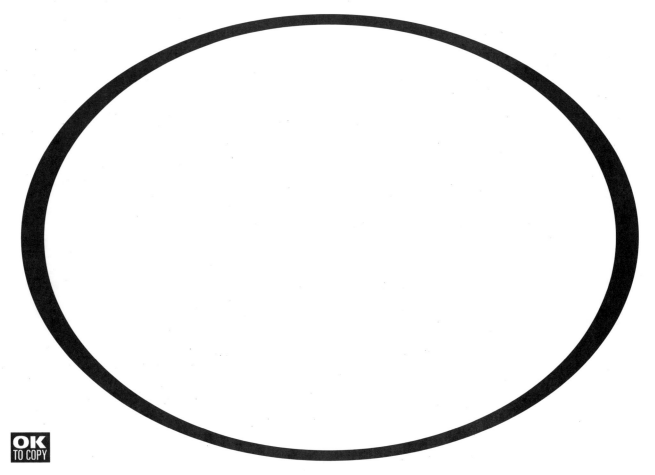

HAT

SHIRT

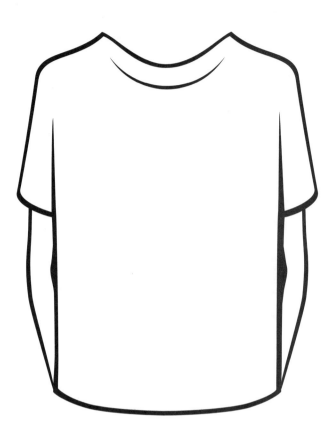

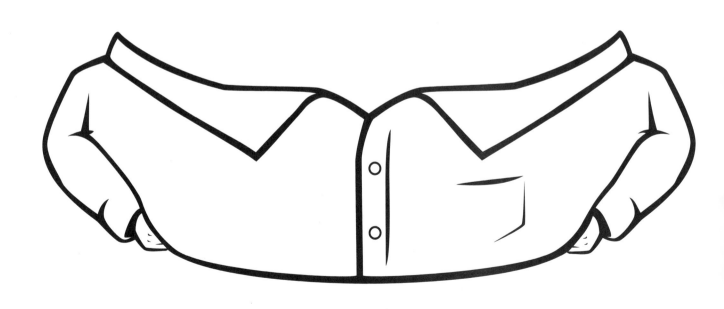

PANTS

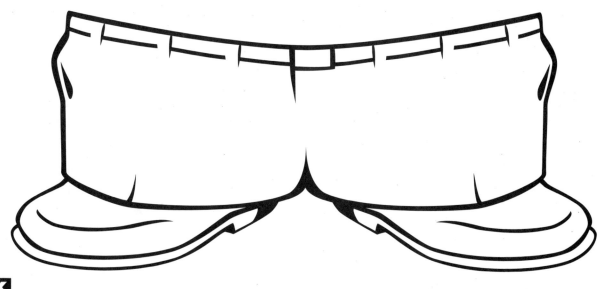

JESUS PERFORMS HIS FIRST MIRACLE

John 2:1-12

Supplies

- "Wedding Jar" handout printed on card stock (2 copies per child) (p. 41)
- stapler
- red construction paper
- spray bottles of water

Easy Prep

- For younger children, tear small pieces of red construction paper so all the kids have enough to cover their jars. Older kids can tear the paper themselves.
- Make a sample craft to show kids.

COLOR-IMPRINTED JARS

What Kids Will Do

Kids make wedding jars.

Discuss Empty Jars

Give each child one "Wedding Jar" handout.

Say: **Our jars are all empty.**

Tell kids one or two ideas you have for filling the jars, such as coloring on them or taping things on them.

Ask:

- **What are some other ways we could fill them?**

Say: **We can fill them in many different ways. But none of those ways would be like how Jesus filled the jars. What Jesus did was a miracle! <u>Jesus used God's power</u> to fill the jars.**

Jesus has God's power.

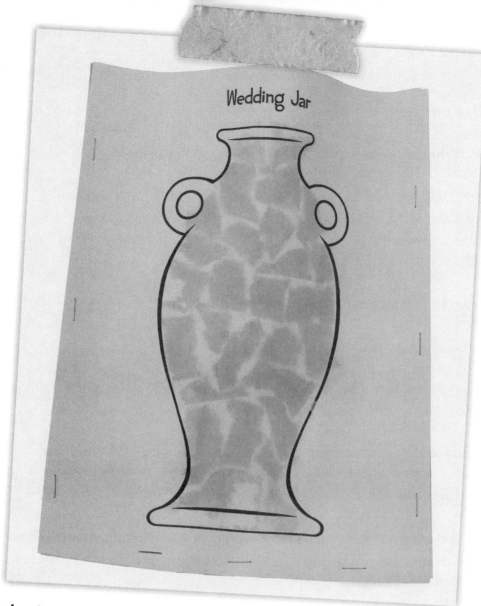

Wedding Jar

Fill the Jars

Say: **Let's fill our jars with colored paper.** Have children arrange the pieces of construction paper to cover their jars. Then have kids spray the construction paper with water.

Ask:

- **What do you think the water will do to the paper?** Share a couple of ways you use water in your daily life.
- **What are some ways you use water?**

Keep the discussion going for at least two or three minutes while the paper dries. Then have children gently pull the paper off to reveal their jars—full of the ink from the construction paper. Then staple a second "Wedding Jar" handout, illustration side facing out, to the back side of the paper with the colored jar. (Staple the sides and bottom, but leave the top open to make a pocket.)

Use the Jars

Ask:

• **What surprised or amazed you about the color?**

Say: **We can use our crafts to tell others about Jesus' amazing miracle.** Help the children tear large pieces of construction paper and crumple them. For each child, open the jar pockets and have kids drop in their crumpled paper pieces.

Say: **Let's tell about Jesus' amazing miracle!**

Lead children to do the following:

Say: **At the wedding, the people ran out of what they were drinking!** Show the empty side of the jar.

Jesus told the servants to take the empty jars and fill them with water. Hold the sides of the jar and march in place to pretend you're carrying the jars to the water.

So the servants filled them with water. But Jesus changed the water into a new, special drink! Have kids turn the jars around to reveal the "filled" jars.

The people poured it out to taste it. Hold the jar upside down, and squeeze the stapled sides in and out to pour out the crumpled pieces of paper.

They said it tasted like the best special drink! Have kids toss the crumpled paper in the air to celebrate.

Lead the children to repeat telling what happened in the Bible story in this way several times.

Say: **In our Bible story, Jesus had the power to make ordinary water into a totally different drink. That's pretty amazing! It was the first time Jesus did a miracle in front of a lot of people, and it showed his friends that <u>Jesus has God's power</u>. Take home your jars and share with others what Jesus did to show that he has God's power.**

WEDDING JAR

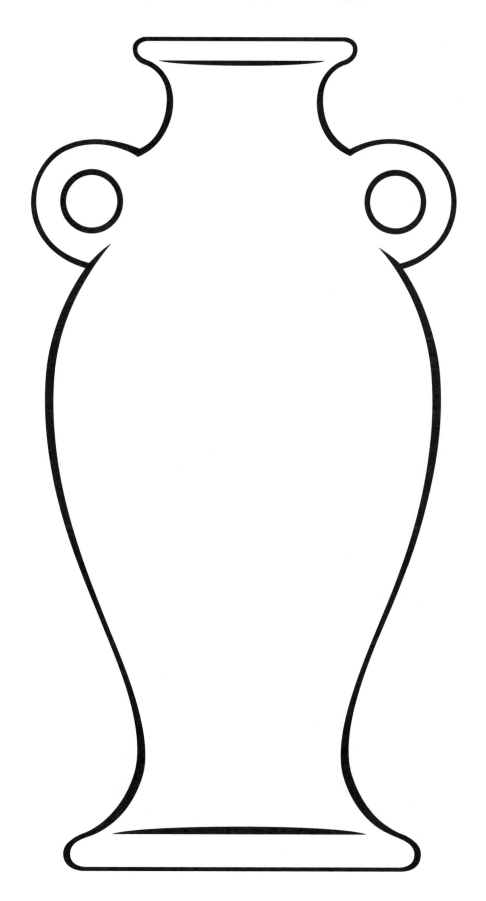

NICODEMUS VISITS JESUS AT NIGHT

John 3:1-21

Supplies

- washable paint in various colors
- paper plates
- disposable circular items such as plastic container lids, paper towel tubes, and various cup sizes
- large plastic tubs or boxes (1 for every 6 kids)
- sheets of white paper (1 per child)

Easy Prep

- Establish a painting area. Put various colors of paint on separate paper plates. There should be enough paint on each plate so kids can dip their circular items in the paint like stamps.
- Gather from your room various toys that are not circular. Combine them with the circular items in the plastic tub or box. If you have more than 1 tub or box, evenly distribute the circular and non-circular items among all the tubs or boxes. Set the tubs or boxes away from the painting area.
- Make a sample craft to show kids.

CIRCLE PAINTINGS

What Kids Will Do

Kids make stamp paintings of circles.

Sort the Shapes

Have about six children gather around each tub or box.

Say: **A circle can remind us that <u>Jesus gives us eternal life</u> with him. A circle is a shape that can help us think of forever because we can't tell where a circle starts or ends.**

Help children look through all the items in their box and pull out all the circular items. After all the circular items are found, have kids take them to your painting area.

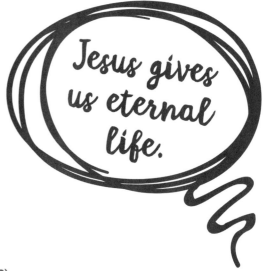

Jesus gives us eternal life.

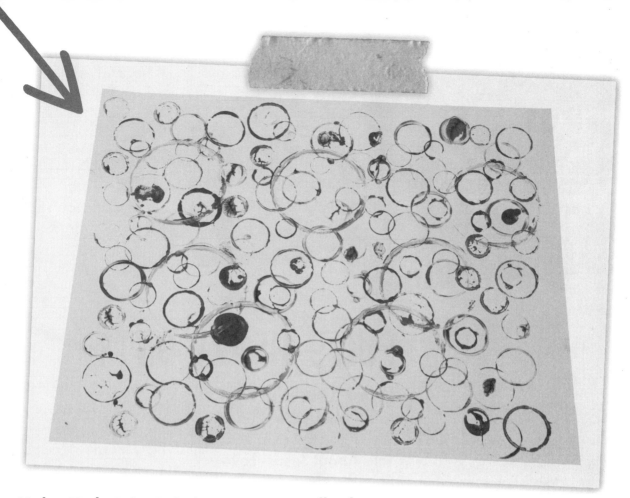

Make Circle-Print Paintings
Give each child a sheet of paper.

Say: **Great job finding all the circles! Remember, circles help us think about spending forever in heaven with Jesus.** Trace your finger in the shape of a circle. **There's no beginning or end to a circle, just like the way we can live forever with Jesus.**

Show kids how to use the circular items as stamps. They can dip the rims of the items in the paint and then press them on their papers. Encourage children to make designs on their papers using the circular prints. Help them share the different circles so kids can make various sizes of circles.

Talk About It
Say: **We can look at circles as a reminder that when we believe in Jesus, we'll live forever with him! Take home your circle painting, and hang it in your room. You can even look for more circles in your home to add to your design—you can ask your family to help you. And whenever you see a circle, you can tell everyone "Jesus gives us eternal life. That means a life that never ends!"**

TIP!

Ages 6-7
Instead of prepping containers of circular objects and other toys for kids to search through, hide the circular items around your room for kids to find. Tell them to look for objects that are made out of lines that don't end.

JESUS IS REJECTED

Luke 4:16–30

Jesus loves everyone.

PUFFY HEART GIFTS

What Kids Will Do

Kids make puffy hearts.

Talk About Jesus' Love

Say: **We know <u>Jesus loves everyone</u> because he said so! The Bible tells us that Jesus' hometown church friends didn't want him to love *everyone*. But <u>Jesus does love everyone</u>, including you!** Show the sample heart craft, and point out that the pictograph says "<u>Jesus loves everyone</u>."

Give a few examples of people *you* know who Jesus loves.

Ask:

- **Tell about someone else you know who Jesus loves.**

Show the sample heart craft again. Say: **Let's make this heart craft to give to someone else. We can tell that person that <u>Jesus loves everyone</u>.**

Tell who you plan to give your heart craft to, and then have the children each choose someone who they want to make the heart craft for.

Make Puffy Hearts

Give each child a heart handout with the pictograph on it. As kids color the hearts, help each child "read" the pictograph that says "<u>Jesus loves everyone</u>."

As children finish coloring the heart handouts, give them each a blank paper heart and have them color those to make the back side of the puffy hearts. (They can also use stickers if you have them.) While children work, staple their hearts together so the decorated sides are facing out. (Staple three edges, leaving the top edge open so kids can stuff them.)

After kids finish decorating, they can stuff the hearts with tissue paper. Staple the final open edge of each heart when it's filled with tissue paper.

Say: **We can always remember that Jesus loves us, and we can share his love with other people. Give your puffy heart as a gift.** Remind children of the people they chose earlier in the activity to give their hearts to. **When you give the gift, tell the person: <u>Jesus loves everyone</u>!**

TIP!

Ages 6-7
Have older kids cut out the heart shapes from the paper after coloring them. Then staple the edges of the hearts together.

JESUS LOVES EVERYONE HEART

JESUS LOVES EVERYONE HEART

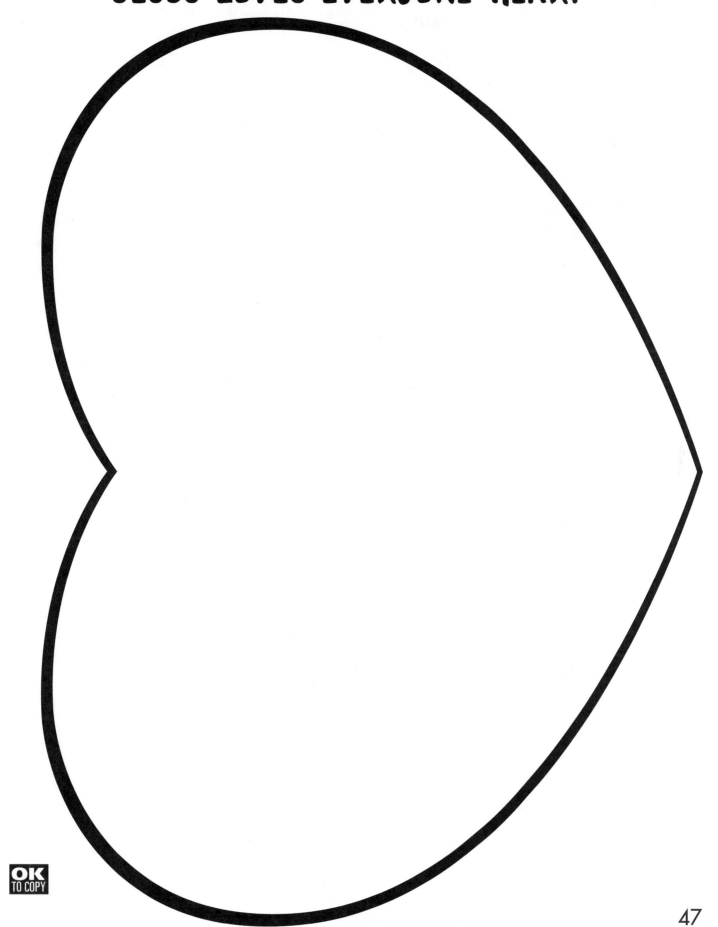

JESUS HEALS PEOPLE

Luke 4:38-40; 5:12-16

Supplies

- "Encouragement Card" handout (1 copy for every 4 kids) (p. 51)
- paper lunch bags (1 per child)
- colorful tissue paper
- glue sticks
- crayons
- stickers
- adhesive bandages (1 per child)
- individually wrapped cough drops (1 per child)
- peppermint or ginger tea bags (1 per child)
- individually wrapped mints (1 per child)

Easy Prep

- Tear several pieces of tissue paper for your youngest children.
- Cut apart the "Encouragement Card" handouts so every child gets 1 card.
- Make a sample craft to show kids.

HEALING CARE PACKAGES →

What Kids Will Do
Kids make care packages for sick people.

Decorate the Bag
Say: <u>Jesus can heal</u> sick and hurting people. **Being sick is no fun. It can make your tummy hurt, make you feel really tired, and even give you a headache or sore throat. And when you're *really* sick, you can feel even worse!**

Let's make care packages for people we know who are sick or hurt. Care packages are special gifts that we make for people to make them feel better. Let kids think about someone they know who may have a cold, or who is in the hospital, or who broke a bone and is wearing a cast.

Say: **To start, we need something to hold all the things we'll put in our care packages.**

Give each child a paper lunch bag.

Say: **We're going to decorate these bags with tissue paper.** Have children tear the tissue paper into small pieces and then glue the pieces onto the paper bags as a mosaic. (Give pre-torn tissue-paper pieces to younger children, if needed.) As kids work, remind them that Jesus can heal people who are sick or hurt. Ask them to talk about other people they know who've been really sick.

Encourage
Say: **Next, let's fill the care packages with things that will help people feel better.**

Have children color the encouragement cards. As they work, talk to them about how when someone we know is sick, we can send them flowers and we can draw them pictures to let them know we love them. Explain that they get to do both with their flower pictures.

Say: **Sometimes sick people get sore throats.** Have kids each put a cough drop in their bag.

Say: **Sometimes people get a bad taste in their mouths if they have a cold or they're sick to their stomachs.** Have kids each put a mint in their bag.

Say: **Sometimes people can have tummy aches when they're sick. Tea can help them feel better.** Have kids each put a tea bag in their bag.

Say: **Sometimes when people get hurt, they need a bandage to help heal the cut.** Have kids each put an adhesive bandage in their bag.

Say: **Our friends or families can use all these things in our care packages when they're sick or hurt, whether they use them right now or they save them for when they need it. They'll definitely feel loved when they get these special care packages from us.**

Help children fold over the tops of the bags, and give each child a sticker to keep the bag closed.

Talk About It
Ask:
* **What helps you feel better when you're sick?**

Say: **I hope our care packages help people who are sick feel better. *We* can't heal people. But we know that Jesus healed a lot of people in the Bible, and he heals people now. <u>Jesus can heal us</u>, too! Let's pray that Jesus will heal the people who get our care packages.**

Lead kids in praying for the recipients of the care packages.

ENCOURAGEMENT CARD

JESUS FORGIVES A PARALYZED MAN

Luke 5:17-26

Supplies

- sheets of paper (1 per child)
- yarn
- pieces of tape or stickers for attaching yarn to paper (4 per child)
- crayons
- markers
- clothespins (1 per child)
- smiley-face stickers (1 per child)
- chenille wires (1 per child)

Easy Prep

- Cut four 1-foot pieces of yarn for each child.
- Make a sample craft to show kids.

BIBLE STORY SET

What Kids Will Do

Kids make mats they can carry a "man" in.

Make a Bible Story Set

Say: **The Bible tells us about a man who couldn't walk. His friends carried him on a mat. Let's make something to help us tell what happened in the story.**

Distribute the clothespins and chenille wires. Lead children to each make the paralyzed man. First, show kids that the clothespin pieces you squeeze can be the legs of the man and the other end of the clothespin can be the head. Have kids lay their clothespins in front of them so they can see both legs, and then have each child place a smiley-face sticker where the head would be. Have each child wrap a chenille wire around the clothespin under the head and twist it to make arms. Encourage kids to use markers to create colorful clothes on the "paralyzed man."

Next, have kids each make a mat for the paralyzed man. Give each child a sheet of paper. While kids color their mats, use tape or stickers to help children attach one piece of yarn to each of the four corners of the paper. (There will be four pieces of yarn attached to each child's mat.)

Jesus forgives us.

Rhyme and Play

Show kids how to place the paralyzed man on the mat and then pick up the mat by holding all four pieces of yarn in one hand. Let them practice balancing the man on the mat.

Have children sit in a circle with their Bible story sets. Say: **Let's use these to tell what happened in the Bible story.** Lead children in acting out what happened. Younger kids can just do the actions, while older children can repeat what you say as they do the actions.

Lay the mat on the ground.

Say: **There once was a man. Let's call him "Stan."** (hold up the man)
He couldn't walk—just lay there like a sock! (place the man on the mat)
Stan's friends loved him so—they carried him to and fro. (use the yarn to pick up the mat)

Took him to Jesus—the one who frees us. (stand up and walk in a circle, carrying the mat)
Lowered him through a roof. I have proof! (lower the mat to the ground)
Jesus forgave him and healed him to the brim. (make the man walk)
Jesus can forgive us, too—yes, me and you! (cheer)

Lead kids in practicing the story several times. If time allows, help them take turns showing what happened to the paralyzed man in the Bible.

A MIRACULOUS CATCH OF FISH

Luke 5:1-11

Supplies

- "Fish" handout (2 copies per child) (p. 57)
- white bath poufs
- white crayons
- thick blue washable markers (1 per child)

Easy Prep

- Cut the ropes off the bath poufs so they stretch out into a long strip of netting. Cut a 1½- to 2-foot strip per child.
- Cut the fish handouts into quarters for younger children. You'll need at least 8 fish per child.
- Make a sample craft to show kids.

FISH MOBILES

What Kids Will Do

Kids make fish and nets to catch them in.

Prepare the Nets

Say: <u>Jesus is amazing</u>! He helped the fishermen catch a *lot* of fish! We're going to make a craft to use to catch a lot of fish. To start, we need to prepare our nets like the fishermen did. Give each child a bath-pouf "net." Have children pretend that they're really fishermen getting their nets ready. Lead kids in carefully stretching out the nets. Show them how they can reach a hand through the netting sleeve and stretch it with their other hand.

Color Fish

Say: **Next, we need some fish!**

Distribute the fish pictures and crayons, and allow time for kids to color.

TIP!

Ages 6-7
Give older kids each two
full-page handouts. Have
them color the fish and
then cut them out.

Catch Fish

Say: **Now it's time to catch the fish in our nets!** Show children how they can "swim" their fish into the nets. Have them practice by putting all the fish into their nets.

Say: **The fishermen tried to catch fish all night, but they didn't catch any! Let's see if you can keep the fish in your net.** Lead children in trying to hold their nets in different ways to see which ways don't lose any fish. They can hold up their nets by each end, or they can hold both ends. Let them experiment and report what they find to the whole group. The nets will do a pretty good job of keeping the fish in, so kids can even try shaking or swinging the nets to see if the fish stay in.

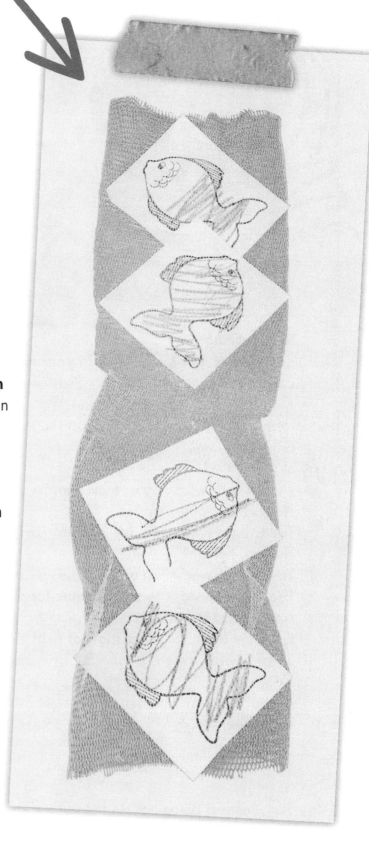

Jesus is amazing.

TIP!

Ages 6-7
Give older children more time to color their fish and experiment with the net rather than singing the song.

Sing a Song
Say: **You caught a lot of fish in your nets! Let's sing a song while we catch some more fish!** Have kids remove the fish from their nets.

Lead children in singing this song to the tune of "The Ants Go Marching."

♪ **The fish go swimming one by one,** *(swim one fish around the net)*
Hurrah, hurrah!
The fish go swimming one by one, *(swim one fish around the net)*
Hurrah, hurrah!
The fish go swimming one by one, *(swim one fish around the net)*
The little one stops to snatch some food; *(touch fish's mouth to the net)*
And the net is lowered down *(push fish into the net)*
From the boat...to catch...lots of fish!
Swish, swish, swish! *(swing net from side to side with fish in it)*

Repeat the verse for each of the eight fish, each time changing the number of fish that you're on and adding another fish to the net at the end.

Sing the song again as time allows.

Say: <u>**Jesus is amazing**</u>**. He helped the fishermen catch a lot of fish! Jesus can help us in amazing ways, too!**

FiSH

WISE AND FOOLISH BUILDER

Matthew 7:24-27

Supplies

- paper lunch bags (2 per child)
- colored construction paper
- sheets of white paper (2 per child)
- glue sticks
- cotton balls (about 5 per child)
- river rocks (about 5 per child, depending on the size)
- crayons
- stapler

Easy Prep

- Cut the construction paper into small squares, each about 1x1-inch. You'll need to cut at least 2 pieces of each color of paper for each child.
- Make a sample craft to show kids.

TRUSTWORTHY HOUSES

What Kids Will Do
Kids make strong houses.

Make Houses
Have each child make two houses out of paper lunch bags. To do this, children will use glue sticks to layer the construction paper squares like bricks on the sides of their paper bags. Children can decorate one or both sides of each house.

Then have each child put five cotton balls in one house and about five river rocks in the other house. Help children fold over the tops of the bags. As you fold the bags, kids can each color two sheets of paper, which will be the roofs for each house. Kids can fold their roofs in half, and you can help them secure the roofs to the bags with one or two staples.

Jesus is trustworthy.

Test the Strength

Say: **Jesus said that we can trust in him. Trusting in Jesus is like building a strong house that won't fall down when the wind blows. <u>Jesus is trustworthy</u>. Let's see which of your houses is stronger.**

Have children blow on their houses, trying to knock them over. The cotton-ball house should fall easily, but the rock house will stand firm.

Talk About It

Ask:

• **Why was one house stronger than the other one?**

Say: **<u>Jesus is trustworthy</u>. When we trust Jesus, we can be like the stronger house you made. When bad things happen, we can still be strong because we trust Jesus to help us and know he will be with us even during hard times.**

Have children take their houses home as a reminder that <u>Jesus is trustworthy</u>.

JESUS EATS WITH SINNERS AT MATTHEW'S HOUSE

Matthew 9:9-13

Supplies

- "Handprint" handout (1 copy per child) (p. 63)
- crayons
- variety of stickers
- stapler

Easy Prep

- Cut the handprints apart.
- Make a sample craft to show kids.

FRIENDSHIP HANDPRINT BOOKS

What Kids Will Do

Kids make books with different handprints.

Color Handprints

Say: <u>Jesus came for everyone.</u> **He even ate dinner with people who were very different from him. We're all different, and it's good to know that Jesus came for all of us!**

One thing that might be different about us is that we have different favorite colors. Ask kids to share what their favorite colors are.

Say: **Wow, you all have such fun, different favorite colors! Even though there are lots of things that are different about each of us, like our favorite colors, <u>Jesus came for everyone</u>—no matter how we are different or the same.**

Distribute four handprints to each child. Have kids color in the hands using their favorite colors.

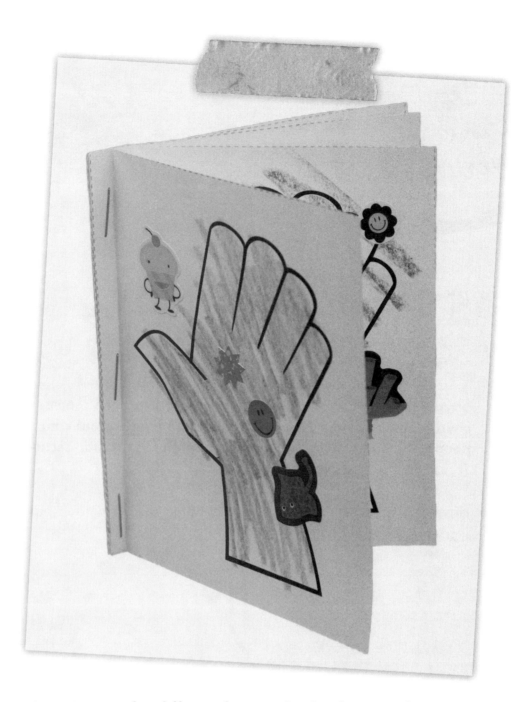

Say: **We are also different from each other because there are different things we like. There are a lot of different kinds of stickers here.** Hold up the stickers. **Use your favorite ones to decorate the hands you colored.**

Make a Book

When children have finished decorating their handprints, have them trade so that they end up with just one of their own handprints and three handprints from other friends. Then staple the handprint sets to make books.

Jesus came for everyone.

Talk About It

Ask:

- What are some differences between the handprints in your book?

Say: **We're all different, but <u>Jesus came for everyone</u>. Some church leaders didn't think Jesus should be hanging out with people who were so different from them. But Jesus did, because <u>Jesus came for everyone</u>.**

Have kids take their handprint books home as a reminder that <u>Jesus came for everyone</u>.

TIP!

Ages 6-7
Instead of using the "Handprint" handout, give older kids each a blank piece of paper. Show them how to fold the paper into quadrants. Have kids each trace a hand to make a handprint in each quadrant. Then kids can color in their handprints and cut apart the quadrants.

HANDPRINT

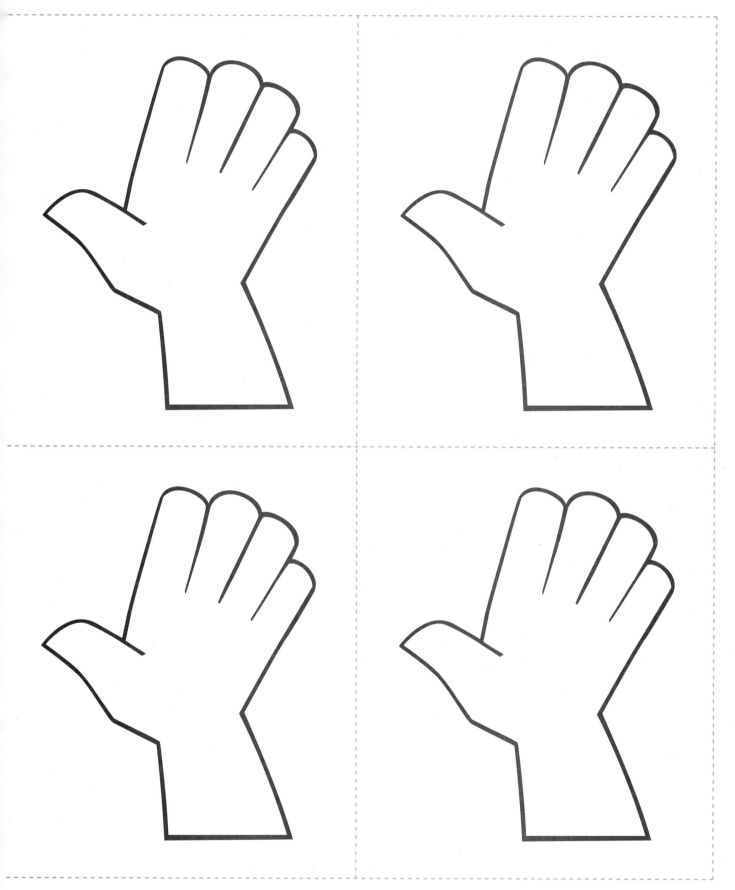

JESUS HEALS A LAME MAN BY A POOL

John 5:1-18

Supplies

- "Man by the Pool" handout printed on card stock (1 copy for every 4 children) (p. 67)
- colored tissue paper
- stickers
- corrugated cardboard
- glue sticks
- tape
- craft sticks (1 per child)
- crayons

Easy Prep

- Cut apart the sections on the "Man by the Pool" handouts.
- Cut pieces of corrugated cardboard to roughly the size of a section you cut from the "Man by the Pool" handout. You'll need 1 cardboard piece per child.
- Make a sample craft to show kids.

STAND UP AND WALK!

What Kids Will Do
Kids make men that can lie down and stand up.

Make the Mat
Say: **One way <u>Jesus showed that he's God</u> was by healing a man who couldn't walk. He made the man better! We're going to make a craft that shows the man before and after Jesus made him better! First, let's make a mat for him to lie on.**

Distribute pieces of cardboard. Have kids tear pieces of tissue paper and glue them to the cardboard to make a colorful mat. Kids can also add stickers to decorate their mats.

Make the Man
Say: **Jesus showed the man that <u>Jesus is God</u>. Let's color the man and then put him on the mat.**
Allow time for each child to color a man from the handout. As kids work, fold their men along the dotted line. Then help kids tape a craft stick to each man so the craft stick sits just above the dotted line on the inside (see photo 1 on page 66).

As kids finish coloring, tape the bottom folded edge of the card stock section to the underside of the mat (align the craft stick with the edge of the cardboard). The craft stick should lean against the cardboard to make the man stand up. Children can practice holding down the man and then letting him go so he "stands up" while they wait for others to finish (see photo 2 on page 66).

Play With the Craft
Have kids play with their crafts as you retell the story. Children can press down the top of their papers to make the man lie down on his mat. When you say, "Stand up and walk," kids can release the papers and the man will pop up.

Jesus is God.

Then have kids continue to play with their mats, and show them how to reenact the story as you sing this song to the tune of "The Farmer in the Dell." Children can sing along with the chorus.

 (Chorus)
My Jesus is God; my Jesus is God. *(hold man down)*
Jesus can do anything *(hold man down)*
'Cause Jesus is God. *(hold man down)*

The man couldn't walk; the man couldn't walk. *(hold man down)*
Jesus said, "Stand up and go." *(let man go so he "stands up")*
Now the man can walk. *(cheer)*

Repeat the song a few times.

Talk About It
Say: **Jesus healed the man because <u>Jesus is God</u>. We can remember that <u>Jesus is God</u> when we play with our crafts and think about the Bible story.**

Have kids take their crafts home as a reminder that <u>Jesus is God</u>.

MAN BY THE POOL

A ROMAN OFFICER DEMONSTRATES FAITH

Luke 7:1-10; Matthew 8:5-13

Supplies

- 20-ounce paper bowls (1 per child)
- "Roman Soldier" handout (1 copy) (p. 71)
- markers or crayons
- foil
- Glue Dots
- hole punch
- chenille wires (2 per child)
- safety scissors

Easy Prep

- Cut pieces of foil in 12x18-inch lengths, 1 per child.
- Punch a hole on opposite sides of each bowl near the rim.
- Make a sample craft to show kids.

ROMAN OFFICER HELMETS

What Kids Will Do
Kids make Roman officer helmets.

Talk About Authority
Say: **The Bible tells us that <u>Jesus has authority over everything</u>.** *Authority* **means being in charge and being able to make the rules.**

Ask:

- **Who are some people who can make rules?** Take a few responses from children.

Say: **A lot of people with authority—people who make rules—wear special uniforms so people know they're important. A uniform is a special outfit to wear while doing a job.**

Let's make special hats called "helmets" that Roman officers wore. Show kids the picture of the Roman soldier.

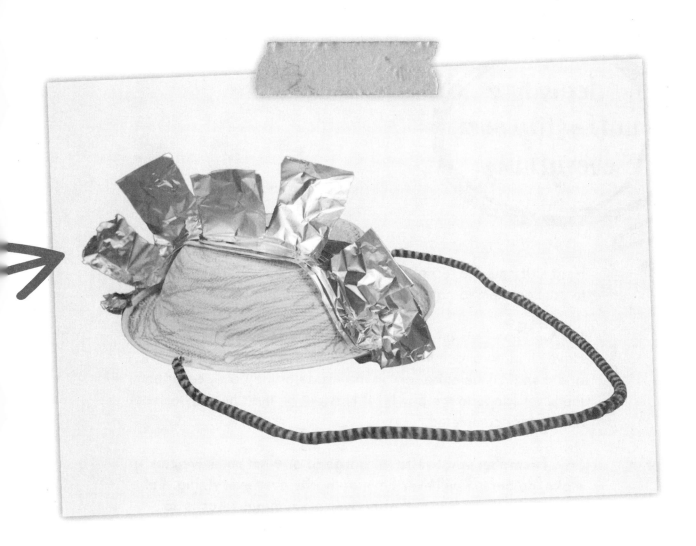

Create a Bowl Helmet

Distribute the bowls and markers or crayons. Invite children to color the bottom and sides of the outside of their bowls.

Guide children to attach the chenille wires to the bowls by inserting one into each hole and twisting it closed. Then have kids twist the two chenille wires together to create the "strap" for the helmet.

Distribute the sheets of foil. Show kids how to accordion fold the foil back and forth into 2-inch-wide pieces, leaving the last 2 inches unfolded. If you have very young children, you may want to prep this for them.

Jesus has authority over everything.

Help kids snip the top of the unfolded piece into "fringe." Be sure to caution them to not cut all the way through.

Put two Glue Dots on the center of the top of each child's helmet. Have children attach the foil strip down the center of the bowl and then tuck the extra foil on the inside of the bowl, securing the silver fringe to the bowl. Let kids put on their helmets as soon as they are completed.

Say: **No matter who we're in charge of or what rules we can make, no person will ever have authority over everything. But Jesus does! <u>Jesus has authority over *everything*</u>! Jesus is *so* strong that he could heal a sick man with just his words.**

Sing a Song
Lead kids in singing the following song to the tune of "London Bridge" as they wear their helmets.

♪ **Jesus has authority.
He's in charge.
He's in charge.
Jesus has authority,
And he loves me.**

Ages 6-7
Let older kids spend more time working on their craft rather than singing the song.

ROMAN SOLDIER

JESUS EASES JOHN'S DOUBT

Matthew 11:1-6; Luke 7:18-23

Supplies

- white trash bags (1 for every 2 kids)
- duct tape (various colors)
- stickers
- clothespins (1 per child)

Easy Prep

- Cut the trash bags along the seams so each bag will make two capes. Cut off any drawstrings.
- Make a sample craft to show kids.

SUPERHERO CAPES

What Kids Will Do

Kids make superhero capes.

Talk About Superheroes

Ask:

- **Tell about your favorite superhero.** Begin the discussion by telling kids who your favorite superhero is and why.

Say: **Superheroes are made up, but in their stories, they rescue people! They can remind us of our *real* rescuer, Jesus! Jesus is the Messiah—a real-life superhero! Let's pretend to be superheroes. We'll make capes and pretend to rescue each other.**

Jesus is the Messiah.

Make Superhero Capes

Give each child half a trash bag. Cut or rip pieces of duct tape in various colors and lengths for kids to decorate their capes with. Show them how to hold the tape so it doesn't get stuck to itself. Kids can also decorate using stickers. It will be easiest for children to do this by spreading out on the floor.

When kids finish their capes, help each child put one on and secure it in front with a clothespin. Then kids can run around the room and try to make their capes fly out.

Play Rescue

Set up various pretend scenarios in which kids need to rescue someone or something.

For example, children could rescue a toy from the floor and put it safely on the shelf. Or they could rescue trash from your craft by putting it in the trash can.

Talk About It

Say: **Jesus doesn't wear a cape, but he's like a superhero because he rescues us. Jesus came to rescue *everyone* because we all need a superhero! <u>Jesus is the Messiah</u>, and he rescues us.**

Have kids wear their capes home as a reminder that <u>Jesus is the Messiah</u>—our real-life superhero.

PARABLE OF THE FARMER AND THE SEED

Matthew 13:1-9, 18-23; Luke 8:4-15

Supplies

- plastic foam bowls (1 per child)
- crayons
- various colors of construction paper, including green
- lollipops (3-4 per child)
- tape

Easy Prep

- Cut green construction paper into rectangles that are roughly 1x3 inches.
- Make a sample craft to show kids.

SWEET FLOWER GARDENS

What Kids Will Do

Kids make flower gardens.

Make Flowers

Have kids tear shapes out of various colors of construction paper. They'll each need about eight shapes. Show them an approximate size and shape to aim for that will fit well on the lollipop as petals, but it's okay if they deviate.

Have children use crayons to decorate their petals. Then have them poke two shapes onto each lollipop stick, followed by a green rectangle. If the pieces slide down, wind tape around the "stem" under the leaves.

Make a Garden

Have each child color an upside-down bowl to be the "garden." Many kids will choose brown or green, but let kids be creative and use fun colors of their choice. Then have kids poke the "stems" through the bowls to make their flower gardens—they should be able to fit four flowers per bowl.

Talk About It

Say: **Just like flowers grow in a garden, <u>Jesus grows us</u>!**

Ask:

• **What are some other things that grow in a garden?**

Say: **A lot of things can grow from seeds. And like some seeds grow into beautiful flowers, <u>Jesus grows us</u> and helps our hearts grow more beautiful and kind. He can help us learn to share.**

Have kids talk about the people they can share their lollipop gardens with. Then encourage children to take their gardens home and share the lollipop flowers.

Jesus grows us.

JESUS DESCRIBES HIS TRUE FAMILY

Matthew 12:46-50; Mark 3:31-35; Luke 8:19-21

Supplies

- jumbo craft sticks (4 per child)
- Glue Dots
- puzzle pieces (larger than a quarter)
- cardboard cut into 5x5-inch pieces (1 per child)
- paper
- pony beads
- crayons
- smiley-face stickers

Easy Prep

- For each child, cut a piece of paper so that it will fit inside a finished frame.
- Make a sample craft to show kids.

FAMILY PHOTO FRAMES

What Kids Will Do

Kids make picture frames.

Make Frames

Say: <u>Jesus wants us in his family</u>! Sometimes families take pictures together and put them in picture frames.

Share about a picture hanging up in *your* house.

Ask:

- **Tell about a picture hanging up in *your* house.**

Say: **We're going to make picture frames so you can put your own family pictures in them!**

Give each child a piece of cardboard and four jumbo craft sticks.

Cut apart individual Glue Dots on the strips, and give them to children. (Adult and teen helpers can help you distribute them.) Help kids put a Glue Dot in each corner of the cardboard, and then show them how to stick a craft stick across the bottom and across the top.

Jesus wants us in his family.

Help them as they add the craft sticks to their cardboard pieces.

Have kids put a Glue Dot in each corner on top of the craft sticks, and then show them how to stick two craft sticks going down the sides. Help them as they add the craft sticks to their cardboard pieces.

Decorate the Frames

Set out puzzle pieces, and have kids use Glue Dots to secure the puzzle pieces all over their frames. Encourage children to use a lot of puzzle pieces and totally cover their frames (see photo at left above).

When kids have finished decorating with puzzle pieces, help each child use a Glue Dot to secure one pony bead at the top center of the back of the frame.

TIP!

Ages 6-7
Give older kids smaller puzzle pieces or colorful buttons to decorate their frames.

This will enable families to hang the frames from a nail through the hole in the bead (see photo at right above).

Add a Picture

Give each child a piece of the paper you cut ahead of time, and set out crayons and smiley-face stickers for kids to share.

Have each child place a smiley-face sticker on the paper for each family member and color pictures to decorate them. Older children can draw bodies on the smiley faces.

Say: **You can hang this picture at home or take a real picture with your family to put in your frame.**

Talk About It
Ask:
• **Tell about the picture you drew.**

Say: <u>**Jesus wants us in his family!**</u> **Just like you're a part of your family, you can be a part of *Jesus'* family! That's a family that's too big to fit in one picture frame!**

JESUS CALMS THE STORM

Matthew 8:23-27 ; Mark 4:35-41 ; Luke 8:22-25

Supplies
- empty 16-ounce plastic bottles (1 per child)
- colorful plastic tablecloth
- stickers
- pony beads
- chenille wires (1 per child)
- transparent tape
- electric fan

Easy Prep
- Cut the plastic tablecloth into 1x15-inch strips. Each child will need 6 strips.
- Make a sample craft to show kids.

Jesus has power to calm storms.

POWER OVER THE WINDSOCK

What Kids Will Do
Kids make windsocks.

Make a Windsock
Say: **Jesus has power to calm storms. In the Bible story, it was very windy on the lake! It was so windy and the waves were *so* big, Jesus' friends got scared.**

We're going to make a craft to remind us that even when it's very windy, Jesus has power to calm storms.

Give kids each a plastic bottle and a few pony beads to put in their bottles, and then help them screw the caps back on. This will help the bottle make noise when the wind blows it.

Set out stickers and plastic strips. Have each child use the stickers like tape to fasten the plastic strips onto a bottle, hanging them from the top of the bottle (see photo at right).

Finally, have each child make a handle for the windsock by taping both ends of a chenille wire to the bottom of the bottle.

Use the Craft

Plug in the fan, and have kids stand near it. Say: **Right now it's calm. There's no wind blowing in our room. But sometimes, storms come!** Turn on the fan, and have kids hold up their windsocks so they blow in the wind. With everyone's windsocks blowing, there should be a very loud noise.

Turn off the fan, and say: **When it's very windy and stormy, we know that <u>Jesus has power to calm storms</u>. Eventually, all storms go away. And then more storms may come.** Turn on the fan again, and have children hold up their windsocks to catch the wind. Then turn it off, and lead kids in saying: <u>**Jesus has power to calm storms.**</u>

Repeat this experience several times, telling kids that storms will come and then turning on the fan. After several times, let kids decide when you turn off the fan by shouting, "Jesus has power to calm storms!" to get you to turn it off.

You can also use this method to tell the Bible story again. As you tell about the boat in the storm, let the windsocks blow in the breeze of the fan.

When you turn off the fan, say: **Jesus said, "Silence! Be still!" <u>Jesus has power to calm storms</u>.**

Ask:

• **Tell what you like or don't like about storms.**

Say: **Take your windsock home and hang it outside as a reminder that <u>Jesus has power to calm storms</u>. When you see or hear it blowing in the wind, you can wait and watch for it to calm down again.**

JESUS HEALS A BLEEDING WOMAN AND RESTORES A GIRL TO LIFE Mark 5:21-43; Matthew 9:18-26; Luke 8:40-56

FIRST-AID KITS

What Kids Will Do
Kids make first-aid kits to take home and use when they're hurt.

Color the Kit
Say: <u>Jesus has power over sickness and death.</u>

Share something your mom, dad, or other family members have done to help you feel better when you're sick.

Ask:

- **What are some things your mom or dad use to help you feel better when you're sick?**

Say: <u>Jesus has power over sickness and death.</u> **He even makes our bodies get better when we get cuts and scrapes! And he gave us things like bandages to help us feel better when we have cuts and scrapes. Sometimes things like bandages come in a first-aid kit. A first-aid kit is a box full of things that can help us get better.**

Show children a first-aid kit. Let them see the things inside as you explain what they can help with.

Supplies
- "First-Aid Kit" handout printed on card stock (1 copy per child) (p. 83)
- a real first-aid kit
- crayons
- stickers
- plastic lacing (a 24-inch length per child)
- transparent tape
- hole punch
- adhesive bandages (5-10 per child)

Easy Prep
- Cut out the first-aid kits, and punch holes where the dots are.
- Make a sample craft to show kids.

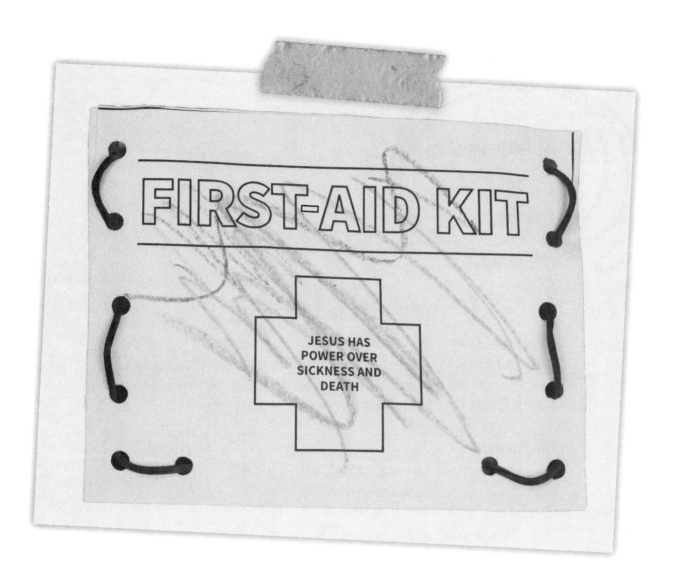

Say: **Let's make our own first-aid kits to remind us that <u>Jesus has power over sickness and death</u>. He can use his power to help us anytime we're sick.**

Give each child a "First-Aid Kit" handout. Set out crayons and stickers, and let kids decorate their kits. As they color, tell kids what the words say so they can remember when they take their kits home.

Sew the Kit
Help kids fold their first-aid kits in half. Then give each child a length of plastic lacing. Hold up a kit so you can show children where to start. Have them poke their lacing through the top hole on one side while you go to each child and tape it in place.

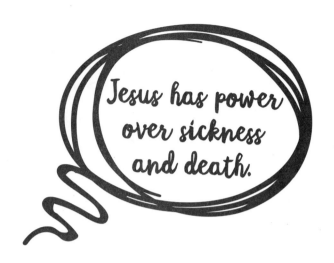

Jesus has power over sickness and death.

Then point out the second hole, and have kids put their lacing through that hole. Continue guiding kids with their lacing in the order of the holes until they make it all the way around their first-aid kits. Then tape the second end in place.

Fill the Kit
Say: **Our first-aid kits are empty! Let's fill them up.** Give kids each 5 to 10 bandages to put in their kits.

Pray: **Thank you, <u>Jesus, that you have power over sickness and death</u>. Thank you for giving us bandages to help us when we're hurt.**

Have kids take home their first-aid kits to use when they get hurt.

FIRST-AID KIT

JESUS HAS POWER OVER SICKNESS AND DEATH

FOLD HERE

JESUS WALKS ON WATER

Matthew 14:22-33; Mark 6:45-52; John 6:16-21

Supplies

- "Jesus and Peter" handout (1 copy per child) (p. 87)
- craft sticks (5 per child)
- blue paper (1 sheet per child)
- small paper plates (1 for every 2 children)
- crayons
- fish stickers (optional)
- tape
- Glue Dots
- stapler

Easy Prep

- Cut each paper plate in half.
- Cut the "Jesus and Peter" handouts apart along the dotted lines so each child will have a copy of the rhyme and an image of Jesus and Peter to color.
- Make a sample craft to show kids.

JESUS AND PETER WALK ON WATER

What Kids Will Do
Kids make Bible story scenes.

Make the Sea
Have kids decorate the blue paper to represent the sea. They can draw waves, fish, seaweed, or other water-related pictures. Provide fish stickers as an optional decoration.

As children finish, fold each paper in half lengthwise with the drawings on the outside and without creasing the fold. Staple the corners of the paper together on each side.

Make a Boat
Give each child Glue Dots, three craft sticks, and half a paper plate. Have kids glue the craft sticks onto the boat to make it look wooden. Then have kids color the wood.

When children finish making their boats, have them glue the boats onto the water, close to the open edge (which is the top of the water).

Make Jesus and Peter Figures

Have kids color their Jesus and Peter figures from the handout. When they finish, help children tape a craft stick to the back of each figure.

Show kids how to place the sticks through the open part of the paper water. Kids should be able to fit their hands in the two openings on either side of the paper and move the sticks around.

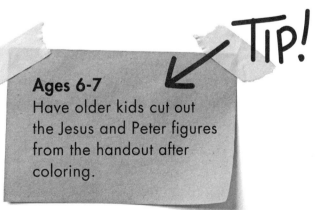

TIP!

Ages 6-7
Have older kids cut out the Jesus and Peter figures from the handout after coloring.

Jesus calms our fears.

Learn a Rhyme

Have kids reenact the Bible story with their crafts as they say this rhyme (say each line first, and then have kids repeat after you).

Some disciples in a boat
Saw a man walking afloat.
They were full of so much fear,
But it was Jesus—"I am here!"

Jesus walked along the waves;
Peter followed, oh how brave!
But he got scared, and then he fell.
Jesus saved him, all was well!

Into the boat the two men climbed;
They worshipped Jesus at that time.
When we're afraid, Jesus is near—
Jesus can calm all our fears!

Repeat as time allows.

TIP!

Ages 6-7
Tell kids they can teach this rhyme to younger siblings or friends to help them remember the Bible story.

JESUS AND PETER

Some disciples in a boat
Saw a man walking afloat.
They were full of so much fear,
But it was Jesus—"I am here!"

Jesus walked along the waves;
Peter followed, oh how brave!
But he got scared, and then he fell.
Jesus saved him, all was well!

Into the boat the two men climbed;
They worshipped Jesus at that time.
When we're afraid, Jesus is near—
Jesus can calm all our fears!

JESUS IS TRANSFIGURED

Matthew 17:1-13; Mark 9:2-13; Luke 9:28-36

Supplies

- "Bright as Light" handout (2 copies per child) (p. 91)
- crayons
- scissors
- tape
- glue sticks
- stapler
- yellow cellophane (you can find this in stores near gift wrap)
- glitter or glitter paint
- paintbrushes (optional)
- aluminum foil

Easy Prep

- Cut an approximately 8x3-inch piece of cellophane for each child.
- Make a sample craft to show kids.

BRIGHT AS LIGHT

What Kids Will Do
Kids make pictures to show how Jesus' appearance changes.

Color the Picture
Give each child a "Bright as Light" handout.
Say: **Before Jesus climbed the mountain with his friends, there was nothing special about the way he looked. He looked like any other man. Color Jesus to look like a regular man.** Set out crayons, and have children color the scene.

Then give the children each a second copy of the handout. Say: **When Jesus was on top of the mountain, the way he looked changed. His friends saw his face and clothes glowing. He didn't look like a regular man then. When his friends saw him like that, they knew he was special. They learned that <u>Jesus is God</u>. I gave you another picture of Jesus. Let's decorate this one to show that Jesus is very special. I brought some supplies that can make him shine and glow the way he did on the mountain.** Have children decorate this picture like they did before, but this time they'll also add glitter or glitter paint to Jesus and tear pieces of aluminum foil and glue them around him to add a shine.

As children work on the second picture,
cut along the dotted lines of each child's first picture.

When kids have finished decorating, help them each tape a
piece of cellophane over Jesus in the second picture.

Attach and Play
Help each child staple the first picture over the second picture.
When kids lift the flap, they'll see Jesus change from an ordinary
man into a shining, glowing Jesus!

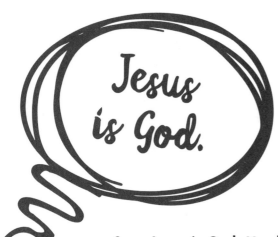

Say: <u>Jesus is God</u>. He showed his friends how bright and amazing God is! We can use our craft to imagine or picture what Jesus' friends saw when Jesus changed from looking like any other man into someone they could tell was God! Let's sing a song that will help us use our pictures to tell others about what happened.

Lead children in singing this song to the tune of "The Farmer in the Dell." Have them lift the flap in their craft as they sing the second verse.

 Jesus was a man,
Jesus was a man,
He hung out with his friends,
'cause Jesus was a man.

Jesus is our God,
Jesus is our God,
His face and clothes shone so bright,
'cause Jesus is our God.

Sing the song a few times.

Talk About It
Say: When Jesus lived here on earth, he looked like a regular person most of the time. Even though he *did* amazing things, he didn't usually *look* amazing. But <u>Jesus is God</u>! His friends got to see that when they saw Jesus shine and glow.

BRIGHT AS LIGHT

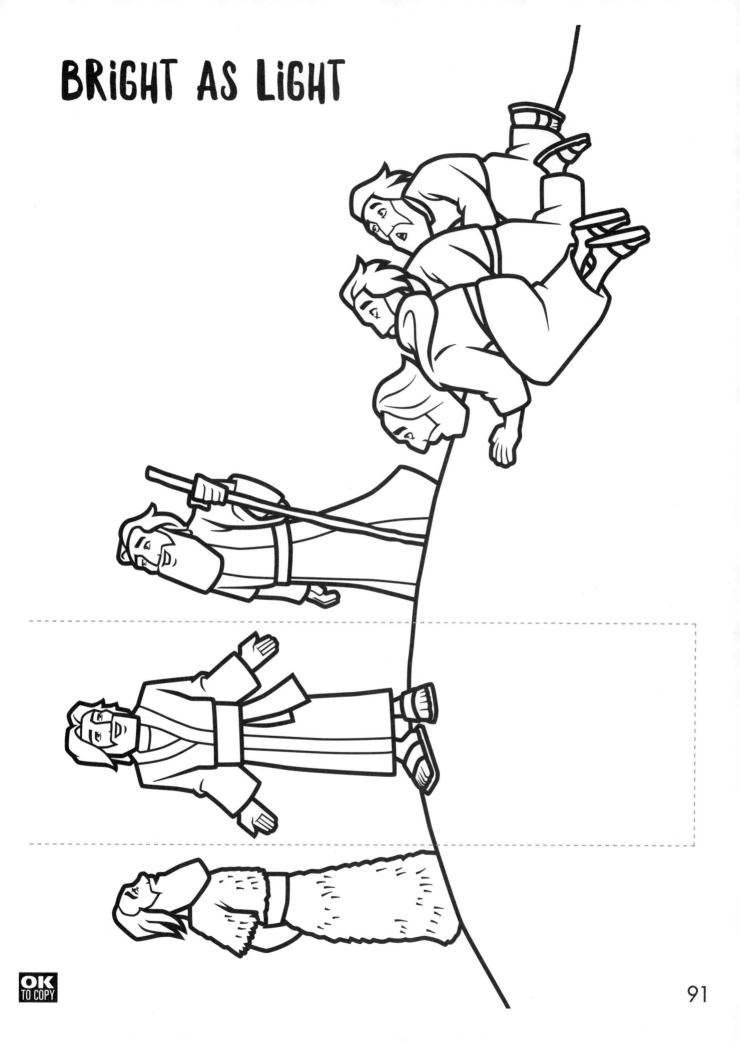

91

PARABLE OF THE GOOD SAMARITAN

Luke 10:25-37

Supplies

- brown paper lunch bags (1 per child)
- "Share Bear" handout (1 copy per child) (p. 95)
- self-sticking googly eyes (½ inch or bigger) (2 per child)
- crayons
- tape
- glue sticks
- newspaper or colored tissue paper
- small prizes such as stickers, preschool-safe bouncy balls, or other fun toys (1 per child)

Easy Prep

- Cut each "Share Bear" handout in half so that each child has a bear front and a bear back.
- Make a sample craft to show kids.

SHARE BEARS

What Kids Will Do
Kids make huggable bears to give away.

Decorate the Bears
Say: **Jesus-followers care for others. Let's make a craft that will help us care for others like the Samaritan did in Jesus' story. The Samaritan helped a man who was hurt and needed extra love. We'll make teddy bears to share with people who need a little extra love!**

Give each child a front and a back of the bear. Allow time for kids to color their bears. Kids can also add self-sticking googly eyes to the bear's face.

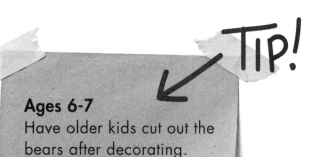

TIP!

Ages 6-7
Have older kids cut out the bears after decorating.

Fill the Bears

Help children shred colored tissue paper or recycled newspaper and fill the paper lunch bags with the pieces. At some point, each child can also put one prize inside his or her bag. When the bag is full, help fold over the top and tape it shut and then help glue the front of the bear to one side and the back of the bear to the other side.

Jesus-followers care for others.

Talk About It

Share something that helps *you* feel better when you're sad.

Ask:

- **What makes you feel better when *you're* sad?**

Say: **Sometimes teddy bears can help us feel better when we're sad.** Show kids how they can gently hug the teddy bear crafts they made.

Say: **Let's find people who seem sad this week and give them bears to care for them. The bears will help the people feel loved. Showing love is a way <u>Jesus-followers care for others.</u>**

Encourage kids to take their crafts home and give the bears to people to show Jesus' love and care.

SHARE BEAR

95

JESUS FEEDS FIVE THOUSAND

Matthew 14:13-21; Mark 6:30-44;
Luke 9:10-17; John 6:1-15

Supplies

- disposable paper bowls (2 per child)
- hole punch
- ribbon
- washable markers
- variety of stickers
- colored construction paper
- chenille wires
- transparent tape

Easy Prep

- Punch a hole in the rim of each disposable bowl.
- Cut a length of ribbon for each child.
- Cut the construction paper into long strips about an inch wide. You'll need 3 to 4 strips of paper per child.
- Make a sample craft to show kids.

SURPRISE BOXES

What Kids Will Do
Kids make surprise boxes.

Make a Box
Say: **Tell about a time you surprised someone with something fun. Maybe you drew a picture to give to your brother or sister, or maybe you and your family surprised your grandma with a fun activity for her birthday. For me…** Tell about a time you were able to surprise someone with something fun and unexpected. Then let preschoolers share.

Say: **It's so much fun to surprise people with good and unexpected things! <u>Jesus does the unexpected</u> and has good surprises for us, too. Let's make fun surprise boxes to remember that we never know what awesome, surprising things God has for us!**

Have each child create a "box" by placing a disposable bowl on top of another one, rim to rim, creating a lid for the bowl. Help children line up the holes on the rims and tie a ribbon through the holes to hold the bowls together. Then kids can decorate the outside of the bowls using the markers and stickers.

TIP!

Ages 6-7
Have older kids make their surprise boxes to give to younger siblings or friends.

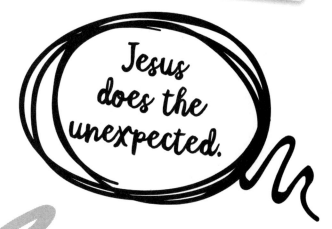

Add a Surprise
Say: **Now that we have our pretty, decorated surprise boxes put together, let's add something surprising and silly inside!**

Show children how to wrap a chenille wire around a finger (or a pen or pencil) to create a spiral shape and how to fold the strips of paper back and forth to create bouncy accordion folds. Let children create several fun shapes with the paper and wires, and help children tape them to the insides the bowls.

Say: **When our boxes are closed, we can't tell that there are fun, silly shapes inside just waiting to pop up when we open the box. Our surprise boxes can help us remember that <u>Jesus does the unexpected</u> and that he has good, surprising things for us!**

Jesus does the unexpected.

DISCIPLES ARGUE ABOUT WHO WILL BE THE GREATEST

Matthew 18:1-6; Mark 9:33-37; Luke 9:46-48

Supplies

- disposable paper bowls (1 per child)
- disposable paper cups (1 per child)
- aluminum-foil sheets (about 4 sheets per child)
- yellow or gold chenille wires (1 per child)
- transparent tape
- Glue Dots
- "You're the Greatest!" handout (1 copy for every 4 children) (p. 101)
- crayons or markers
- variety of stickers

Easy Prep

- Cut the handouts along the dotted lines so that you have 1 section per child.
- Cut the chenille wires in half.
- If you're using a roll of aluminum foil rather than pre-cut foil sheets, cut the foil into about 12-inch lengths, creating several sheets per child.
- Make a sample craft to show kids.

THANK-YOU TROPHIES

What Kids Will Do
Kids make trophies.

Talk About Trophies
Ask:

- **When do people get trophies?** Younger children might not have an answer, and that's okay. Simply let children have a chance to tell, if they know.

Say: **We might get a trophy when we're the best at something—maybe we're on a soccer team or T-ball team that won a big game or we're dancers who gave a great performance. We give trophies to people to tell them that they are great. But Jesus shows us what it really means to be great. Being great like Jesus doesn't mean that we're the best at something or that we won a contest; being great means that we love and serve each other like Jesus did!**

Ask:

- **Who is someone you know who is great like Jesus? You might tell about someone who loves you and helps you.** Share your own example first of someone who loves and helps you.

Say: **Let's thank those special people by making them thank-you trophies!**

Put the Trophy Together

Give kids each a cup and a bowl, and show them how to cover each with aluminum foil. Children need to cover only the outside of the bowl, but they can cover the entire cup in foil. Then help children turn their bowls upside down and use several Glue Dots to attach the bottom of the cup to the bottom of the bowl.

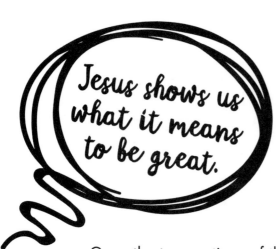

Jesus shows us what it means to be great.

Once the two sections of the trophy are glued together, help kids use tape to secure a section of chenille wire to each side of the cup by taping one end of the wire at the top of the cup and the other end of the wire near the bottom to form a handle shape.

Add a Note

Say: **Now let's add a special note that you can place inside the trophy to thank the person you're giving your trophy to.** Hold up a section of the "You're the Greatest!" handout. **This says: "You're the greatest! Thank you for loving and serving like Jesus!" If you are giving this trophy to one of your parents, I can help you write "mom" or "dad" on the note, and you can color on the note and add stickers to it.**

Give each child a section of the "You're the Greatest!" handout, and let kids color and decorate it however they want. When children have finished, help them fold the note and place it inside the cup portion of the trophy.

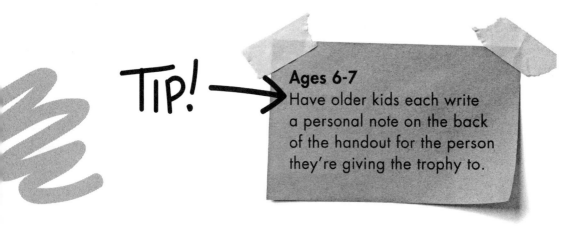

TIP!

Ages 6-7
Have older kids each write a personal note on the back of the handout for the person they're giving the trophy to.

YOU'RE THE GREATEST!

"YOU'RE THE GREATEST! THANK YOU FOR LOVING AND SERVING LIKE JESUS!"

"YOU'RE THE GREATEST! THANK YOU FOR LOVING AND SERVING LIKE JESUS!"

"YOU'RE THE GREATEST! THANK YOU FOR LOVING AND SERVING LIKE JESUS!"

"YOU'RE THE GREATEST! THANK YOU FOR LOVING AND SERVING LIKE JESUS!"

JESUS FORGIVES A WOMAN

John 8:1-11

Supplies

- "Jesus Forgives Board" handout (1 copy per child) (p. 105)
- construction paper in a variety of colors
- transparency sheets or plastic sleeve protectors (½ sheet per child)
- stickers, foam shapes, colorful pompoms, or other craft supplies
- transparent tape
- Glue Dots
- washable markers
- wet wipes

Easy Prep

- Cut the transparency sheets or plastic sleeve protectors in half horizontally so that each child will have half a sheet.
- Cut a few sheets of construction paper into 1x8-inch strips so each child can have about 4 strips.
- Make a sample craft to show kids.

DRY-ERASE BOARDS

What Kids Will Do
Kids make dry-erase boards.

Talk About Jesus Erasing Our Sin
Say: <u>Jesus forgives us.</u> **We all make bad choices and do wrong things, and bad choices and wrong things are called** *sin.* Draw a sad face on your sample craft using a washable marker. **But when we ask Jesus to forgive us for bad choices we make, it's like he erases our sins!** Use a wet wipe to wipe away the sad face you drew. **They disappear! Our craft will help us remember that <u>Jesus forgives us</u>.**

Jesus forgives.

Make Dry-Erase Boards

Give each child a "Jesus Forgives Board" handout, and read the sentence on the handout for kids.

Give kids each half a transparency, and have them use tape to attach it to the handout.

Then children can use tape or Glue Dots to add strips of construction paper around the clear sheet to make a colorful border.

Jesus forgives.

Once children have added their borders, let them decorate the construction-paper frames using the craft supplies and Glue Dots.

While children work, talk about how they are adding fun, bright, happy decorations to their boards. Then talk about how we can feel knowing that <u>Jesus forgives</u> us—happy, full of God's joy, and so on.

Once kids have finished, let them color on the erasable portion of the boards with washable markers. Give them wet wipes so they can erase their pictures when they are done, like Jesus erases our sins.

JESUS FORGIVES

JESUS VISITS MARY AND MARTHA

Luke 10:38-42

Supplies

- paper grocery bags (1 per child)
- decorating supplies such as stickers, markers, and crayons
- cotton balls, cotton batting, scrap fabric, or wadded-up newspaper
- duct tape
- stapler
- reflective worship music (optional)
- music player (optional)

Easy Prep

- Keep the paper grocery bags flat and unopened, and secure the folded bottom section to the side of the bag using duct tape so the bag can't be opened all the way. Prep 1 bag for each child.
- Make a sample craft to show kids.

CHAT MATS

What Kids Will Do

Kids make chat mats.

Talk About Chatting With Our Friends

Say: **Spending time with friends is so much fun— playing together, watching movies, eating snacks, exploring outside! And something we do with our friends during all those activities is talk together.**

Ask:

- **What are some things you talk to your friends about?** Share your own example first, such as talking about new movies you've seen, what you're making for dinner, or how you're excited for an upcoming trip.

Say: **Someone else we can talk to about all of those things is Jesus! Even though we can't see him, we can talk to Jesus about anything because <u>Jesus wants to be our friend</u>.**

This craft is called a chat mat! Show the sample craft. **Our craft can remind us that we can chat with Jesus anytime and about anything! He wants to hear everything you're thinking, because Jesus is your friend.**

Make the Chat Mats

Give each child a paper grocery bag, duct-taped side down, and let kids decorate the tops of the bags however they wish with the provided supplies. While children work, help them talk about why they like knowing that Jesus wants to be their friend.

Once children have finished decorating, let them place cotton balls or another type of stuffing inside the bag to give their mats plenty of cushioning. When they've added enough stuffing, help children fold over the opening of the bag and staple it closed.

Chat on the Mats

As kids finish their mats, have them each find a place in your room to sit on their chat mats with a friend who has also finished. Have pairs chat about what their favorite games are to play with their friends. After everyone has finished, say: **When Jesus visited Mary and Martha, Mary sat at Jesus' feet and listened to everything Jesus said. Let's practice listening to Jesus right now, too!**

Have children each find a place in the room to sit on their chat mats, away from other children. If you like, turn on reflective music and dim the lights, and have kids spend a minute or so talking and listening to Jesus.

You can also have children lie on their stomachs on their mats with their heads down so they can avoid being distracted while listening to Jesus.

After about a minute, turn off the music and have children share if they heard Jesus say anything to them. You can also ask children how they felt while they prayed, and tell kids that feelings of peace, love, or warmth are also a way Jesus lets us know he is with us.

Jesus wants to be our friend.

JESUS HEALS A CRIPPLED WOMAN

Luke 13:10-17

Supplies

- colored felt (1 sheet per child)
- "Person Shape" handout printed on card stock (1 copy) (p. 111)
- plastic straws (1 per child)
- colorful yarn (16-inch length per child, plus extra for decorating)
- large googly eyes (2 per child)
- Glue Dots
- washable markers
- decorating supplies such as foam shapes and stickers
- transparent tape
- permanent marker
- hole punch

Easy Prep

- Cut out the person shape to use as your template. Using a permanent marker, trace the person shape onto a piece of felt and cut out the felt person shape with scissors. Create 1 felt person for each child.
- On each felt person shape, use the hole punch to make a hole at the top of each arm and at the top of the head.
- Cut 3 lengths of yarn for each child—two 6-inch lengths and one 4-inch length.
- Make a sample craft to show kids.

FELT-PEOPLE MARIONETTES

What Kids Will Do

Kids make marionettes.

Make the Marionettes

Say: **The Bible tells about a time Jesus healed a crippled woman. Her back was hunched over, and she couldn't stand up straight for a long, long time. But Jesus made her better—and she could stand up straight! Let's make a craft that will remind us of how Jesus helped the woman.**

Give each child a felt person shape. Let kids decorate their people by adding two googly eyes and pieces of yarn for hair and coloring a mouth with the washable markers. They can also add any other decorations they like using the provided supplies.

Once children have added the decorating elements to their felt people, help them tie the end of each 6-inch length of yarn through the punched holes in the felt person's arms and then tie the 4-inch length of yarn through the hole at the top of the head. When the three pieces of yarn have been tied through the holes, help children tape the other ends of the yarn to a drinking straw to create the marionette handle.

Act Out the Bible Story
Once children have finished making their marionettes, lead kids in acting out the Bible story with their craft.

Say: **A long time ago there was a woman who was crippled. Her back was hunched over, and she couldn't stand up straight—for years and years and years! Everywhere she went she was bent over.**

Ages 6-7
For older kids, print the "Person Shape" handout onto several sheets of card stock (about 1 for every 5 kids) and cut out the person shapes to use as templates. Let kids trace the shapes onto felt with permanent markers and then cut out the felt person shape with scissors.

TIP!

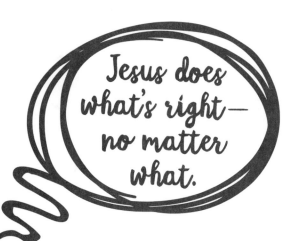

Jesus does what's right— no matter what.

Have children walk their marionettes around by holding the handle of the marionette above the ground or table so that only the top half of the marionette is in the air while the lower half rests on the flat surface.

Say: **The woman was probably in a lot of pain! What sound do you make when something hurts?** Pause. **But then Jesus saw the woman at church. And he called out to her, "Dear woman, you are healed of your sickness!" And then Jesus touched her and she was better—she could stand up straight!** Have children raise their marionettes so that just the bottoms of the feet touch the ground. **The woman thanked God for healing her! Shout out something the woman might have said when she was thanking God for healing her.** Help kids think of things they could say, such as "Yay," "Thank you, God," and "Wow!" Let them "run" their felt people around to show how excited the woman was.

Say: **Some people didn't think that Jesus should have healed the crippled woman, but Jesus knew the woman needed help right then. <u>Jesus does what's right—no matter what!</u>**

TIP! →

Ages 6-7
Rather than leading older kids in acting out the story, challenge kids to act out the Bible story without your help.

PERSON SHAPE

111

JESUS HEALS A BLIND MAN

John 9:1-41

Supplies

- black construction paper (⅓ sheet per child, plus extras)
- transparency sheets (about ¼ sheet per child)
- "Sunglasses" handout printed on card stock (1 copy) (p. 115)
- permanent marker
- white crayons
- stickers
- transparent tape
- safety scissors

Easy Prep

- Cut out the sunglasses shape to use as your template. Then use a permanent marker to trace the sunglasses shape onto a transparency sheet 4 times, or as many as will fit, and cut out each sunglasses shape with scissors. Cut out 1 sunglasses shape for each child.
- Then use the same template to trace the sunglasses shape multiple times onto sheets of black construction paper using a white crayon. Cut out 1 black sunglasses shape for each child.
- For each child, cut 2 strips of black paper that are about 4 inches long and 1 inch wide.
- Make a sample craft to show kids.

BLIND-TO-SEE SUNGLASSES

What Kids Will Do
Kids make sunglasses.

TIP!

Ages 6-7
Cut the sheets of black construction paper into thirds, and give one section to each child. Let kids use the transparency sunglasses shape as a template to trace the shape onto the black paper with a white crayon and then cut it out.

Make the Sunglasses
Say: **The Bible tells about a man who had been blind ever since he was born. Because he couldn't see, the man couldn't work, so he had to beg people for food and money. But <u>Jesus has the power to heal</u>, so he healed the man and helped him see for the first time ever! Let's make a craft that will remind us what Jesus did.**

Give each child a black construction paper sunglasses shape, and let kids decorate the front of their sunglasses by coloring them with white crayons and adding stickers. While kids work, ask them about what they are thankful they can see, such as the colors of the sunset, the peaks of mountains, or the smile of a friend (see photo 1 on page 114).

When children have finished decorating their sunglasses, give them each one of the sunglasses shapes that you cut from a transparency. Help them tape together the straight top of both cutouts, making sure the black paper is on top of the transparency. Make sure kids don't tape together the sides or bottoms of the cutouts (see photo 2 on page 114).

Then have children turn their sunglasses over so that the transparency side is on top, and help them tape one strip of black paper to each side of the clear transparency to create the sides of the frames. To make the frames sturdier, you can give each child four strips of paper instead of two so kids can tape two pieces together for each side (see photo 3 on page 114).

Jesus has the power to heal.

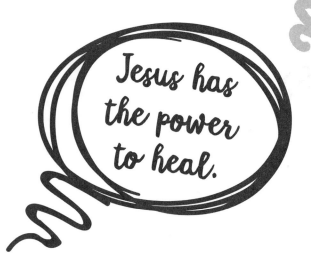

Bible Story Reminder With the Glasses

Once children have finished making their sunglasses, have them put their sunglasses on while you say the following rhyme and they listen for your instructions. Remind them that because the sunglasses will be covering their eyes, they will have to listen closely to know what to do.

There was a man who could not see,
(have children shake their heads "no")
But in Jesus he believed!
(have kids give a thumbs-up)
Jesus put mud on his eyes,
(have kids put their hands over their eyes and sunglasses)
A wash in the river—oh surprise!
(have kids hold their hands up as if in surprise)
The man could see—it was real.
(have kids lift up the black paper portion of their glasses)
Jesus has the power to heal!
(have kids cheer)

Repeat as time allows.

SUNGLASSES

JESUS CLAIMS TO BE GOD'S SON

John 10:22-42

Supplies

- large paper cups (1 per child)
- permanent markers (optional)
- craft supplies such as stickers, foam shapes, colored pompoms
- Glue Dots
- ribbon (two 24-inch lengths per child)
- transparent tape
- stapler
- smocks

Easy Prep

- Cut out the bottom of each paper cup.
- Make a sample craft to show kids.

Jesus is God's Son.

MEGAPHONE HATS

What Kids Will Do
Kids make crafts that are two things in one.

Make the Megaphone Hat
Say: <u>Jesus is God's Son.</u> When Jesus lived here on earth, he was a person like you and me—he ate dinner, slept, and talked and laughed with his friends. Even though Jesus was like us, Jesus is also so much more! And that's because <u>Jesus is God's one and only Son!</u> Wow! That means Jesus is two things at the same time—he is a person, and <u>he's God's special Son.</u>

Our craft is two things at the same time, too! Hold up the sample craft. **It's a megaphone that helps make our voices loud** (shout through your sample craft). **And it's also a fun hat we can wear** (put the sample craft on top of your head). **Our craft can help us remember that Jesus is two things—a man and <u>God's special Son!</u> Let's get started!**

Have kids put on smocks. Give each child a paper cup, and allow kids to decorate the cups with the permanent markers (if used) and craft supplies. While kids work, remind them that Jesus was a man but also God's special Son. And tell children that in a way, we are more than one thing, too.

A child may be a girl but also a daughter, a sister, a friend, a cousin, a soccer player, a really good artist, and so on. Tell kids some of the ways you are two things, and then have them share ways they are two things in one, too.

When they've finished decorating their cups, give kids each two sections of ribbon and help them tape one end of each length of ribbon to each side of the cup near the wide rim. (The wide rim of the cup is the base of the hat, and the end that was cut out is the megaphone side.) Once children have taped on their ribbons, you can staple each ribbon to the cup for a little extra support.

When children have finished making their crafts, have each child try the craft out by putting on the hat and then shouting through the megaphone, "Jesus is God's Son!"

TIP!

Permanent markers are used in this craft for kids to color their cups, as crayons won't show up and washable markers will easily smudge on waxy paper cups. If you're concerned about younger children coloring with permanent markers, you can easily leave out this part of the craft.

PARABLES OF THE LOST SHEEP AND LOST COIN

Luke 15:1-10

Supplies

- "Lost Coin & Sheep Game Board" handout (1 copy per child) (p. 121)
- colored construction paper (1 sheet per child, plus extras)
- crayons or washable markers
- transparent tape

Easy Prep

- Cut apart 1 handout for each child. Use the dotted lines as a reference for cutting apart the game board portion and the pictures of the coins and sheep.
- Cut colored construction paper into squares that are about 2x2 inches. Each child will need 8 squares.
- Make a sample craft to show kids.

LOST COIN & SHEEP GAME BOARDS

What Kids Will Do

Kids make game boards.

Make the Game Board

Say: **Jesus loves us so much and wants to be our friend! That's why <u>Jesus looks for us</u>! Just like the man who looked for his lost sheep and the woman who looked for her lost coin, <u>Jesus looks for us</u>.**

Show the sample craft and say: **Let's make a seek-and-find board game. When you're finished making your game, you'll get to hide pictures of coins and sheep under the colorful squares** (demonstrate hiding the pictures on the sample craft), **and a friend will have to guess which squares the lost coins and sheep are hiding under!**

TIP!

Ages 6-7
Let older kids cut apart the handout and the 2x2-inch construction paper squares.

Lost Coin & Sheep Game Board

Give each child a sheet of construction paper and the game board template you cut apart from the handout. Help children tape the game board to the sheet of construction paper. Then kids can each pick out eight construction-paper squares to tape over the square outlines on their game boards. Help children tape down only one side of each square, and make sure they tape each square on the same side so that all the squares lift in the same direction.

Once children have taped down the game board template and the eight construction-paper squares, let them color and decorate their game boards and the coin and sheep game pieces.

Jesus looks for us.

Play With a Friend!

When kids have finished making their game boards, have them each find a partner to play the game with. Children can take turns by having one child hide the four coin and sheep pictures under the colored squares while the other child turns away or closes his or her eyes.

Kids can then play in one of two ways: by simply guessing which squares have something hidden under them until all four pieces have been found, or by playing a memory game and having to correctly guess which two squares have the matching coins and the matching sheep.

Depending on time, have children play one or both versions of the game. Make sure kids each get a chance to use their game board to hide the coins and sheep as well as a turn to guess using the other child's game board.

Say: **You can remember that just like you looked for the hidden coins and sheep on your friend's game board, <u>Jesus looks for us</u>, too!**

LOST COIN & SHEEP GAME BOARD

PARABLE OF THE PRODIGAL SON

Luke 15:11-32

Supplies

- paper bowls (2 per child)
- "Jesus Loves You! Hearts" handout (1 copy for every 2 children) (p. 125)
- pink chenille wires (1 per child)
- pink pompom balls (1 per child)
- small pink pompom balls, sections of pink chenille wire cut into pieces, pink foam shapes, or pink construction paper cut into triangles (2 per child)
- googly eyes (2 per child)
- Glue Dots
- markers or crayons

Easy Prep

- Cut out the hearts on the "Jesus Loves You! Hearts" handout along the dotted lines.
- Punch a hole in the rim of each paper bowl in about the same spot on each of the bowls so that the holes line up with one another.
- Make a sample craft to show kids.

PIGGY HEART BANKS

What Kids Will Do

Kids make piggy banks filled with reminders for their friends and families of Jesus' love for them.

Make the Pig

Say: **Jesus told a story about a dad and his son, who ran away from home. The son spent all the money that his dad had given him, so he ended up living and working with dirty, smelly pigs! Even though his son spent all the money and had a yucky job, the dad still loved his son and was so happy when he came home. And we can know that <u>Jesus loves us no matter what</u>, too! Let's make a piggy craft to remind us of Jesus' story!** Show kids the sample craft.

TIP!

Ages 6-7
For older kids, cut the handouts in half and give each child half a page so kids can cut apart the hearts themselves.

Give each child two paper bowls, and have kids decorate the body of the pig by coloring the outsides of the bowls. You can suggest they color the body pink, and they can even add brown mud spots on their pigs.

Once children have finished coloring the bowls, help them line up the two holes, making a dome shape with one bowl on top of the other. Help children put a pink chenille wire through the two holes, bend the wire in half, and twist the two sides of the wire several times to secure it to the bowls and keep the bowls tied together. Then help kids twist the doubled-up wire around a finger to give their pigs curly tails.

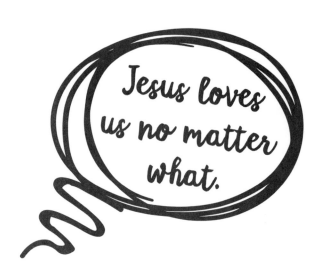

Jesus loves us no matter what.

Next, help children use Glue Dots to secure two googly eyes onto the pig and a pink pompom ball as a snout. Then help them add two ears, using small pompom balls, pieces of chenille wire, pink paper, or whatever supply you have on hand.

Say: **Your pigs are looking so good! Now I have something for you to add to the inside of your pig—like a piggy bank.** Show children the heart cutouts, and tell them that the words say "Jesus loves you!" **<u>Jesus loves us no matter what</u>! And that can make us feel so happy! But other people might not know that <u>Jesus loves them no matter what</u>, too. So when one of your friends or family members seems sad or has had a hard day, you can give the person one of these hearts as a reminder of how much Jesus loves them!**

Have kids color the hearts and then put them inside their pigs. While children are coloring, have them tell who they could give one of the hearts to.

JESUS LOVES YOU! HEARTS

JESUS RAISES LAZARUS FROM THE DEAD

John 11:1-44

Supplies

- paper bowls (1 per child)
- jumbo craft sticks (1 per child)
- "Lazarus" handout (1 copy for every 2 children) (p. 129)
- thick yarn or ribbon (about 6 feet per child)
- crayons and markers
- Glue Dots
- transparent tape

Easy Prep

- Prep a Lazarus template for each child by cutting along the dotted lines.
- Turn the paper bowls upside down, and cut an angled opening into the side of each paper bowl for the tomb "entrance." You can make the opening approximately 2 inches wide at the roof (base of the bowl) and about 4 inches wide at the rim of the bowl, which will sit on the ground.
- Cut an approximately 6-foot length of yarn or ribbon for each child.
- Make a sample craft to show kids.

WRAPPED LAZARUS

What Kids Will Do

Kids make Lazarus craft sticks and paper-bowl tombs.

Wrap Lazarus

Say: **Jesus' friend Lazarus died, and all his friends and family were so sad. Even Jesus was sad and cried because his friend had died. But <u>Jesus has power over death</u>, and he brought Lazarus back to life! Jesus' power is amazing!**

Give each child a craft stick and a "Lazarus" template. Have children color the picture of Lazarus, and then help them fold the picture of Lazarus in half along the solid line. Help children secure the picture around one end of the craft stick by placing Glue Dots along one side of the craft stick and attaching the "front" picture of Lazarus to the stick (see photo 1 on page 128).

TIP!

Ages 6-7
Have older kids cut out the picture of Lazarus and the tomb entrance from the bowl.

Then help kids turn the stick and paper over and place Glue Dots along the other side of the craft stick before folding the "back" picture of Lazarus over the stick and securing it to the Glue Dots as well (see photo 2 on page 128).

Once the picture of Lazarus is folded over and glued to the craft stick, give each child a section of yarn or ribbon and help kids tape one end of the yarn to the craft stick just below the Lazarus picture. Then show children how they can wrap the yarn around Lazarus to cover him and hide the picture.

Make the Tomb

After children have each finished making their Lazarus, give each child a paper bowl and have kids color it to look like a tomb. You can suggest they draw rocks, grass, flowers, trees, or any other elements they want around the outside of the bowl.

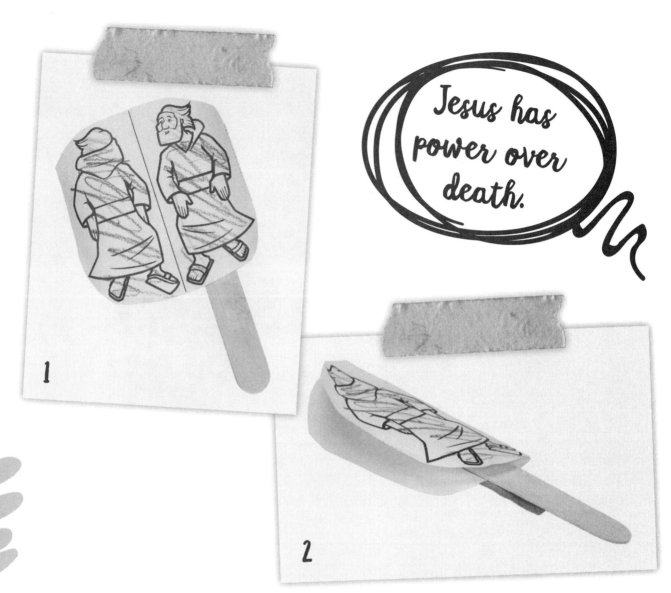

Jesus has power over death.

Act Out the Story

Say: **When Lazarus died, his family wrapped his body in cloth, kind of like how we wrapped our Lazarus in yarn. Then his family buried him by placing his body in a tomb, which was like a cave in the side of a hill.** Have children slide their wrapped Lazarus craft sticks inside the opening of the tomb bowls. **Lazarus' body was in the tomb for four days.** Have children count to four with you. **Then Jesus came. Jesus shouted, "Lazarus, come out!" And Lazarus did! He walked out of the tomb, and his friends and family helped him unwrap the cloth from his body. He was alive again!** Have each child take the Lazarus figure out of the tomb and unwrap the yarn covering the picture of Lazarus. **Jesus is so amazing—he has power over death!**

LAZARUS

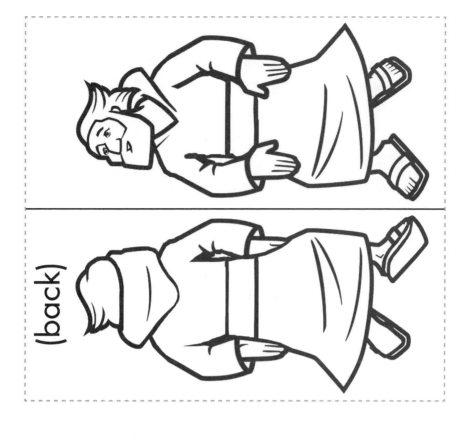

(back)

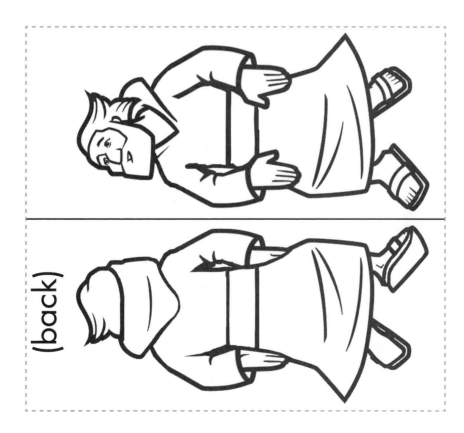

(back)

JESUS HEALS TEN MEN OF LEPROSY

Luke 17:11-19

Supplies

- white paper plates (2 per child)
- colored crepe paper streamers or ribbon
- small pony beads
- crayons
- craft supplies such as stickers and foam shapes
- transparent tape
- glue sticks
- stapler

Easy Prep

- Tear or cut the crepe paper streamers or ribbon into 6-inch sections. Prepare about 10 lengths per child.
- Make a sample craft to show kids.

Jesus deserves our thanks.

THANKFULNESS TAMBOURINES

What Kids Will Do

Kids make tambourines to praise Jesus.

Make a Tambourine

Say: **Jesus deserves our thanks,** and one way we can thank Jesus is by singing! Lots of times when we sing, we sing along with music. So let's make a fun musical instrument called a *tambourine* that we can use to celebrate and thank Jesus! Show children the sample craft.

Give each child two paper plates, and distribute crayons. Have kids turn both paper plates upside down and color the bottom side of the plates. Then children can add stickers, foam shapes, or any other craft supplies you have on hand.

When children have finished decorating the outsides of the plates, have them turn one of the plates over, and help them tape the lengths of streamers or ribbon around the inside rim of the plate. Then help kids add a small handful of beads to the center of the plate. Remind children not to put any beads in their mouths.

TIP!

Ages 6-7
Give older kids each a 5-foot section of paper streamer or ribbon, and let them use scissors to cut it into smaller pieces as they make the craft.

While children are working, point out howmany fun, bright, different colors they are using to decorate their craft. Ask each child what his or her favorite color is, and point out that God made that beautiful color.

After kids have each taped streamers and added beads to one of the plates, help them place the second plate on top of the other, creating a slight dome shape with the decorated sides of the plates facing out. Then staple the rims of the plates together so that no beads fall out.

Musical Praise
Say: **Music and singing are a great way to say thank you to Jesus. Let's thank Jesus now by singing and using our tambourines to make fun music!**

Have children sing this song to the tune of "Ten Little Indians" while playing with their tambourines.

**Thank you, thank you, thank you, Jesus.
Thank you, thank you, thank you, Jesus.
Thank you, thank you, thank you, Jesus.
You deserve our thanks!**

Repeat a few times.

TIP!

Ages 6-7
Have older kids sing a worship song they're familiar with as they play their tambourines.

JESUS BLESSES THE CHILDREN

Matthew 19:13-15; Mark 10:13-16; Luke 18:15-17

Supplies

- knee-high nylons (1 per child) (you can find value packs with 20 individual nylons for about $6 at stores such as Walmart and Target)
- cotton balls or cotton batting
- tan rubber bands (1 per child)
- felt or scrap cloth (1 large piece, about 12x12 inches, per child)
- colored markers (permanent markers will work best)

Easy Prep

- Make a sample craft to show kids.

NYLON BABY DOLLS

What Kids Will Do

Kids make their own baby dolls.

Make Baby Dolls

Say: **Jesus loves kids so much—you're so important to him.** Show children the sample craft. **You're each going to make a baby doll of your own to take care of. Your baby doll can help you remember how much <u>Jesus wants to be with children.</u>**

Set out the cotton filling, and give each child a knee-high nylon. Help children fill the nylon with cotton, pushing the cotton toward the toe end of the nylon.

Once children have filled about 3-4 inches of the toe section of the nylon with cotton, help them tie a rubber band around the nylon just below the cotton filling—the toe section of the nylon will become the baby doll's head.

Then children can continue to loosely fill the "body" portion of their baby dolls with cotton, stopping when there is about 2 inches of unfilled nylon left at the end.

Jesus wants to be with children.

Tie the end of the nylon into a simple knot so that the cotton filling stays inside.

While kids work, ask if they have any younger brothers or sisters and how they help their parents care for them. If children don't have younger siblings, you can also ask how they help care for a pet or a special doll or stuffed animal at home.

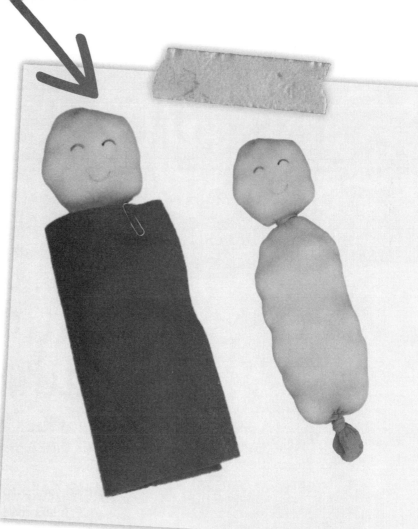

Once children's nylons have been filled and tied off, showthem how to gently pull the nylon and cotton to the sides to smooth out the lumps and flatten the cotton—this will help give the doll's head and body more of a flattened circle and oval shape rather than a rounded ball shape. Then each child can use markers to draw the doll'sface, including eyes, a nose, mouth, and even hair.

Finally, children can wrap their baby dolls in pieces of felt or cloth as baby blankets.

Say: **Children matter so much to Jesus! When we show love to other kids, we're showing Jesus' loving care to them! We can care for a toy doll to practice showing Jesus' love, or we can help care for a baby brother or sister. When you care for a doll or you help your parents care for a baby brother or sister, you can remember how much <u>Jesus loves and wants to be with children!</u>**

TIP!

Ages 6-7
Older kids can make this craft to give to a younger sibling or friend. Remind kids that sometimes it can be hard to have patience with kids who are younger than they are. But Jesus wants us to be kind and welcoming to them, too, because Jesus cares for children.

If time allows, let the children practice different ways to care for the baby dolls they made. For example, they can pretend to rock, feed, and sing to their baby dolls.

JESUS HEALS BLIND MEN

Matthew 20:29-34; Mark 10:46-52; Luke 18:35-43

Supplies

- thin cardboard (or chipboard) cut into 2½x6-inch pieces (1 per child)
- aluminum foil cut into 2x2½-inch pieces (1 per child)
- colored construction paper cut into 2½x6-inch pieces (2 per child)
- green dot color coding stickers (1 per child)
- red dot color coding stickers (1 per child)
- small gem stickers
- crayons or washable markers
- Glue Dots

Easy Prep

- Make a sample craft to show kids.

"CALL ON JESUS" CELLPHONES

What Kids Will Do
Kids make cellphone crafts.

Make Cellphones
Say: **Jesus loves when we talk to him, and we can know that <u>Jesus always hears us</u>.**

One way we talk to people is on a phone. Let's make phones to remind us that we can talk to Jesus and <u>he hears us</u>. Show children the sample craft.

Have each child choose two pieces of construction paper, and give kids each a piece of cardboard. Help kids apply Glue Dots to each side of the cardboard and then attach a piece of construction paper to each side.

TIP!

Ages 6-7
Rather than covering their cellphones in colored construction paper, have older kids use colorful duct tape to cover the cardboard.

Jesus hears us.

Then help children each fold their cardboard in half to look like a flip phone.

Help children use Glue Dots to attach the aluminum foil to the top half of the phone for the "screen." On the bottom half of the phone, have kids add green dot and red dot stickers for the "call" buttons and jewel stickers as the keys. Once children have added the sticker keys, they can decorate the backs of their phones using crayons or markers.

When children have finished making their cellphones, have them pretend to call Jesus on their phones and have a conversation with him.

Say: **Jesus heard the blind man who called out to him to be healed, and <u>Jesus always hears us</u> when we call out to him, too!**

TIP!

Ages 6-7
Invite older kids to pray to Jesus as they pretend to talk to him through their cellphones.

135

JESUS MEETS ZACCHAEUS
Luke 19:1-10

Supplies
- plastic spoons (1 per child)
- index cards (1 per child)
- crayons or markers
- colored yarn
- googly eyes (2 per child)
- permanent markers
- Glue Dots
- transparent tape
- safety scissors
- reflective worship music
- music player

Easy Prep
- Using the photo on page 139 as a guide, follow these instructions to prepare an index card for each child: Fold an index card in half so that the card is almost a square shape. Make sure the writing lines are folded toward the inside. Then cut each card to look like a robe or shirt. In the middle of the fold, cut out a small "V" shape about an inch across. Then on each side of the card about halfway down, cut about half an inch in, and then make two angled cuts down toward the corners of the folded card.
- Cut one 6-inch piece of yarn for each child, which will be the prayer pal's belt.
- Make a sample craft to show kids.

PRAYER PALS

What Kids Will Do
Kids make prayer pals.

Make Prayer Pals
Say: **Zacchaeus learned that <u>when we spend time with Jesus, he changes us</u>! That's true for us, too!** Show children the sample craft. **We're going to make a "Jesus" prayer pal. When you go home, you can put your prayer pal next to your bed or even by your sink in the bathroom. Every time you see your prayer pal, it can remind you to spend time with Jesus! You can spend time with Jesus while you brush your teeth in the morning** (have children pretend to use a toothbrush) **or when you play outside** (have children pretend to throw a ball) **or even when you watch cartoons and eat a snack** (have children pretend to eat). **Jesus is always with you, and <u>when we spend time with Jesus, he changes us</u>!**

Give each child a prepared index card, and have kids draw on it with crayons or markers to look like clothes for their prayer pals. Remind children they can color on both sides of the index card.

When kids have finished coloring, give them each a plastic spoon, and help them slide the index card up the spoon handle toward the bowl of the spoon. Then help them tape the index card in place by securing the bottom of the index card to each side of the handle with a small piece of tape.

TIP!

Ages 6-7
Give each child a whole index card. Show kids how to fold the index card in half and then cut out the shirt shape by referring to the sample craft and/or photo.

When we spend time with Jesus, he changes us.

Children can each add two googly eyes to the prayer pal's face using Glue Dots (the outer, convex side of the spoon will be the front of the face). Have them draw a smile using a permanent marker.

Finally, help children each tie a 6-inch length of yarn around the prayer pal as a belt. Let children use safety scissors to cut pieces of yarn for hair. They can use Glue Dots to attach the yarn hair to their prayer pals.

Spend Time With Jesus

When kids have finished making their prayer pals, have them take the prayer pals and find a spot to sit in your room, spreading out so they aren't sitting near anyone else.

Say: **Our prayer pals can remind us to spend time with Jesus. Let's spend some time with Jesus right now!** You can have children lie down or cover their eyes so they aren't distracted during the prayer time.

Softly play a worship song, and pray: **Dear Jesus, thank you for loving each of us so much. You're a friend who is always with us. Help us be more like you so we can share your love with others.**

Thank you for always wanting to spend time with us and always hearing us when we talk to you—even right now. Encourage children to spend time quietly talking with Jesus as the worship music plays. After a minute, slowly fade out the music.

Say: **Jesus loves when you spend time with him, and you can remember that <u>when we spend time with Jesus, he changes us</u> and makes us more like him!**

JESUS' TRIUMPHANT ENTRY

Matthew 21:1-11; Mark 11:1-11; Luke 19:28-40; John 12:12-16

Supplies
- paper bowls (1 per child)
- 3-ounce paper cups (1 per child)
- craft sticks (1 per child)
- "Donkey" handout (1 copy per child) (p. 142)
- "Jesus" handout (1 copy) (p. 143)
- gray or brown markers or washable paint
- paintbrushes (optional)
- black, gray, or brown yarn
- crayons
- transparent tape
- Glue Dots
- safety scissors

Easy Prep
- Cut a small slit the width of the craft stick just below the lip of each cup. Then turn over the bowls and cut the same size slit near the curve at the bottom of the bowls.
- For younger children, cut out the donkey face shape from the handout. Let older kids cut out the shape by themselves.
- Cut several 3-inch lengths of yarn for each child.
- Cut the mirrored Jesus figure from the "Jesus" handout and fold in half along the dotted lines.
- Make a sample craft to show kids.

BOWL & CUP DONKEYS

What Kids Will Do
Kids make donkey crafts.

Make Donkeys
Say: **When Jesus entered Jerusalem, he rode on a donkey instead of a fancy horse. People lined the streets praising Jesus because <u>Jesus is the King!</u> Let's make a donkey craft to remember this Bible story.** Show children the sample craft.

Give each child a bowl, cup, and craft stick. Have kids paint or color the craft stick and the outside of the bowl and cup brown or gray. Then give children the image of the donkey face and have them color it with crayons.

Once children have finished coloring all the elements of their donkeys, help them put their crafts together. Help kids slide the craft stick through the slits in the bowl and cup and tape the craft stick to the inside of each to hold it in place (the craft stick will be the donkey's neck). Then help children tape the circle on the donkey's face to the opening of the cup (the cup will become the donkey's nose). Finally, let kids tape or glue several pieces of yarn to the other side of the bowl as the donkey's tail.

When children have finished making their crafts, let them take turns putting the Jesus figure on the back of their donkeys. They can push the donkeys across a table and shout, "Hosanna to the King!"

Jesus is the King.

DONKEY

142

JESUS

143

THE POOR WIDOW'S OFFERING

Mark 12:41-44; Luke 21:1-4

COIN WRISTBANDS

Supplies

- colored construction paper
- large plastic coins (1 per child)
- washable markers
- stickers
- clear packing tape
- Glue Dots or glue sticks
- transparent tape

Easy Prep

- Cut the construction paper into strips about 1½x7 inches long. Make 1 paper strip for each child.
- Make a sample craft to show kids.

What Kids Will Do

Kids make coin wristbands.

Make Wristbands

Say: **A poor woman gave Jesus two coins when she was at church. Two coins doesn't seem like a lot, but Jesus loved her gift! Other people gave more money, but this woman gave what she had with a happy heart—and <u>Jesus loves givers</u> who have happy hearts!** Have children each make a heart shape with their hands.

We can remember that even if we don't feel like we have a lot, we can still share what we *do* have with other people. We can share our toys with our sisters, brothers, or friends; we can spend time with someone who might be sad; or we can even just share a smile. Let's make a coin wristband to remember that <u>Jesus loves givers</u> like the woman who gave what she had. Show children the sample craft.

Jesus loves givers.

Give each child a strip of paper and a plastic coin. Help children each glue a plastic coin to the middle of the paper, which will be the wristband. Then children can decorate the paper strip by coloring and adding stickers.

When they're finished decorating, place a piece of clear packing tape over each entire wristband so that it won't tear and so that the plastic coin stays in place. Help children put the bands around their wrists and tape the bands together with a piece of transparent tape.

Point out that there's only one coin on each wristband, and the woman in the Bible story didn't have very much either...but she gave what she had to God with a happy heart!

TIP!

Ages 6-7
Let older kids each cut out the wristband from the construction paper, making sure it will wrap all the way around their wrists.

THE PLOT TO KILL JESUS

Luke 22:1-6; Matthew 26:1-5, 14-16;
Mark 14:1-2, 10-11

Supplies

- washable markers
- spray bottle filled with water
- "Double Heart" handout (1 copy per child) (p. 149)
- safety scissors

Easy Prep

- For each 3- and 4-year-old child, fold the "Double Heart" handout and cut out the heart so when you unfold the paper, there are two connected hearts.
- Make a sample craft to show kids.

HE'S SAD WITH US

What Kids Will Do
Kids make heart crafts that "cry."

Make a Double Heart
Say: <u>Jesus knows what it's like to be hurt by a friend.</u> One day, Jesus' friend Judas decided not to be a good friend to Jesus anymore. He really hurt Jesus. When we're hurt, sometimes we say that our heart hurts. Show children a "Double Heart" handout that hasn't already been cut out.

Share about a time you felt hurt; then explain that your heart hurt.

Say: **Think about a time you felt hurt or a time you could say your heart hurt.**

Give each child a "Double Heart" handout. Give 3- and 4-year-olds a folded, pre-cut heart, and give older kids an uncut one and show them how to fold the page on the center line. Have kids use the markers to color on one heart as they think about a time they felt hurt. You can also encourage them to talk about times they felt hurt without naming any specific people.

Say: **Jesus knows what it felt like in those times you felt hurt.**
Cut a folded "Double Heart" handout without cutting through the
place where it's joined to the other heart. You want two attached
hearts after you unfold the paper. Have 3- and 4-year-olds open
their pre-cut hearts to reveal the two hearts, and help older
children cut their hearts to create the same effect. **When our
heart hurts, Jesus' heart knows what it feels like!**

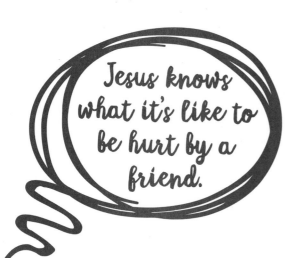

Jesus knows what it's like to be hurt by a friend.

Encourage children to color the second heart. Then say: **We might cry when our heart hurts.** Lightly mist a colored heart. **When we feel hurt, we cry. And Jesus is sad with us.** Lightly mist the other colored heart to ensure the ink is "crying" on both hearts. **Jesus knows what it's like to be hurt by a friend. See? It looks like there are tears falling down our hearts now.**

Pass the spray bottle around to the children, and have them take turns spraying their hearts. As kids each spray their hearts, encourage them to say, "Thank you, Jesus, for being sad with me."

Say: **Jesus doesn't want us to stay sad. He *does* know what it's like to be hurt by a friend, but he wants to help us feel better.** Point out how the "color tears" made something beautiful. **Look at how the sad tears turned into something beautiful. When Jesus is our friend, he helps us feel better. That's because <u>he knows what it feels like to be hurt by a friend</u>.**

DOUBLE HEART

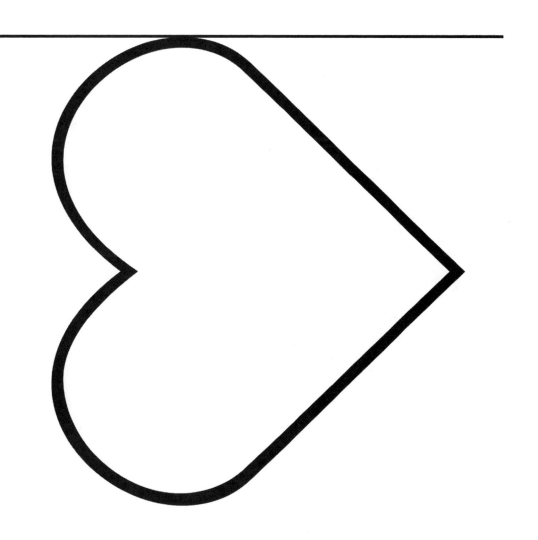

JESUS WASHES HIS DISCIPLES' FEET

John 13:1-17

Supplies
- white paper tablecloths lined with plastic (1 for every 16 kids)
- washable paint in a variety of colors
- disposable bowls
- small paintbrushes
- ribbon
- smocks or large T-shirts (optional)

Easy Prep
- Cut the tablecloths into approximately 1x1-foot squares. Make 1 square for each child.
- For each square, cut a small slit in each of the top corners. You'll help children tie a length of ribbon through each slit as the apron strings.
- Cut two 18-inch lengths of ribbon for each child.
- Pour washable paint into the disposable bowls, and put a couple of paintbrushes in each bowl.
- Make a sample craft to show kids.

SERVING APRONS

What Kids Will Do
Kids make serving aprons.

Make an Apron
Say: **One time Jesus wrapped a towel around his waist and served his friends by washing their feet. Sometimes people who serve wear aprons around their waists. If you go out to eat at a restaurant with your family, the server who brings you your food probably wears an apron. Maybe you and your parents wear aprons when you cook dinner or bake cookies at home.**

We're going to make aprons to remind us of how Jesus served and that we can serve others, too.

Have children put on smocks or large T-shirts if you have them. Then give each child a tablecloth square, and let kids decorate their aprons with the washable paint. Once children have finished painting their aprons, allow the aprons to dry completely.

After the aprons have dried, help children tie a length of ribbon through each of the slits at the top of the aprons. Then help kids put on their aprons by tying the pieces of ribbon around their waists.

Jesus shows us how to serve.

Talk About It

Say: **Jesus showed us how to serve** when he wrapped a towel around his waist and washed his friends' feet. We can wear our aprons while we serve, just like Jesus!

Ask:

- **What's a way you can serve your family this week while you wear your apron?**

Help children come up with ideas for how to serve their families this week while wearing their aprons. Kids might help set the table, help a parent unload the dishwasher, or clean the doorknobs.

TIP!

Make sure to buy paper tablecloths that are lined with plastic on the back. This will ensure that the paint won't bleed through the paper.

JESUS IS BETRAYED AND ARRESTED

Matthew 26:47-56; Mark 14:43-52;
Luke 22:47-53; John 18:1-11

Supplies

- paper towel tubes (1 per child)
- markers
- stickers
- 2-feet lengths of yarn (1 per child)
- stapler
- transparent tape

Easy Prep

- For each child, cut the paper towel roll in half, and then bend each cardboard tube along the length. Hold the 2 creased portions together and staple them together along the length of the tubes to create a heart shape.
- Make a sample craft to show kids.

HEART BiNOCULARS

What Kids Will Do
Kids make heart binoculars.

Make Binoculars
Say: **Jesus loves everybody! Jesus loves each one of us...he loves children, grown-ups, people who are sick, people who don't know about Jesus at all, and people who love Jesus back! But <u>Jesus also loved his enemies</u>—the people who weren't very nice to Jesus and didn't like him at all. Jesus showed love to everyone, even the people who were mean to him. Let's make a craft to remember to show Jesus' love to everyone we see!** Show children the sample craft, and point out how the shape of the binoculars kind of looks like a heart.

Jesus loves even his enemies.

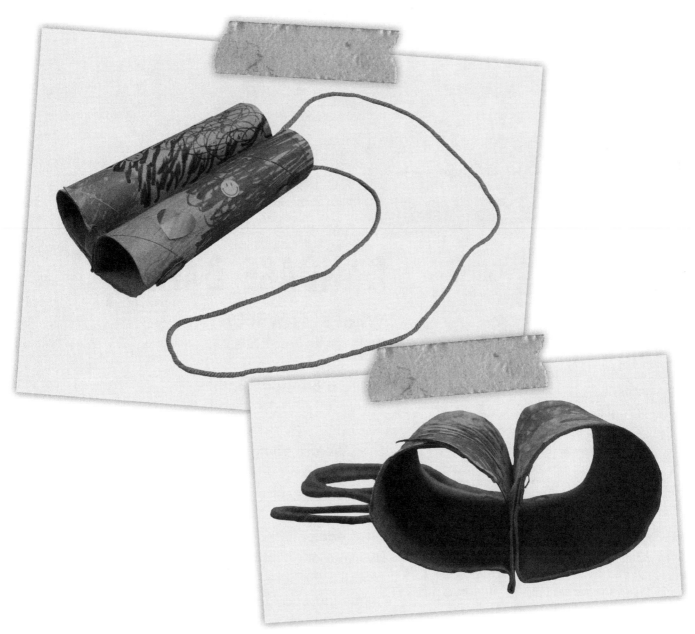

Give each child a pair of cardboard binoculars, and let kids decorate their binoculars using the markers and stickers. Once kids finish decorating their binoculars, help them tape each end of a length of yarn to the bottom edge of the cardboard tubes.

Have children put the yarn "straps" over their heads and look around the room through their binoculars. Whenever children see someone through their binoculars, have them tell that person, "Jesus loves you!"

Say: **Just like <u>Jesus loved even his enemies</u>, our heart binoculars can remind us to show Jesus' love to everyone we see!**

JESUS IS PUT ON TRIAL

Matthew 27:15-31; Mark 15:6-15;
Luke 23:1-25; John 18:28-19:16

Supplies

- paper lunch bags (1 per child)
- sheets of newspaper (1 per child)
- aluminum foil (a few sheets per child)
- colored painter's tape or duct tape

Easy Prep

- Tear off strips of painter's or duct tape in 4- to 5-inch lengths, and stick them to the side of a table for children to easily grab. You can also tear the tape into smaller widths, if desired, for more variety and to make the tape go further.
- Make a sample craft to show kids.

BANDAGE BALLS

What Kids Will Do
Kids make toy balls.

Make a Bandage Ball
Show children the sample craft.

Say: **We are going to make a ball we can play with. Our craft will help us remember that <u>Jesus understands suffering</u>. Let's get started.**

Give each child a paper lunch bag and a sheet of newspaper. Help children open the paper bag and crumple the sheet of newspaper and then place it inside the bag. Then have kids crumple the entire paper bag as tightly as they can—this will be the middle of the ball. Next, help children wrap the crumpled bag in a few sheets of aluminum foil to form a round ball shape.

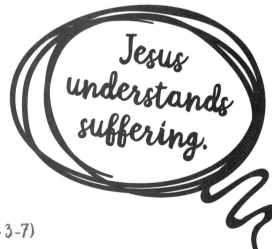

Jesus understands suffering.

While kids work, talk about how the aluminum foil feels a little bit pokey and prickly.

Say: <u>Jesus understands suffering.</u> **Even though Jesus never did anything wrong, people who didn't like Jesus hurt him. They hit him and put sharp, pokey thorns on his head that felt kind of like how this foil feels pokey.**

Once children have covered their balls with foil, help them cover the outside of their balls with strips of tape.

Say: **The strips of tape sort of look like bandages, which we might use when we get hurt really badly.**

Jesus was hurt lots of times in our Bible story.

After kids have finished their craft, they can play with their balls in your room by kicking them around or tossing them back and forth with a friend.

Say: **Jesus might have felt kind of like your ball when he was hurt. People put him in jail and were rough with him. They hurt him a lot. When you feel hurt or thrown around like a ball—like when someone says something unkind to you or someone hits you—you can remember that <u>Jesus understands your suffering.</u> He knows what it feels like to be hurt, and he is there with you!**

JESUS IS CRUCIFIED
Matthew 27:32-61; Mark 15:21-47; Luke 23:26-56; John 19:17-42

Supplies
- transparency sheets (1 per child)
- "Stained Glass Window Template" handout (1 copy) (p. 159)
- colored tissue paper, including red
- white glue
- paintbrushes
- disposable bowls
- yarn
- hole punch

Easy Prep
- Copy the "Stained Glass Window Template" handout onto the transparencies.
- Cut the tissue paper into 1-inch squares. Keep the red tissue paper squares separate from the other colors.
- Cut a 2-foot length of yarn for each child.
- Pour glue and a small amount of water into the disposable bowls so the watered-down glue can easily be "painted" onto the transparencies.
- Make a sample craft to show kids.

STAINED-GLASS WINDOWS

What Kids Will Do
Kids make stained-glass windows.

Make a Stained-Glass Window
Give each child a transparency sheet with the images of the heart and cross printed on it.

Say: **Jesus loves us...a lot! Hearts are something that can remind us of love.** Have children trace the outline of the heart on their transparency sheets using their fingers. **And Jesus loves us so much that he died for us on a cross. We all do wrong things sometimes. But Jesus loves us and forgives us for those things when we ask him to. Jesus' love brings color and happiness and joy to our lives! He takes away our sins so we can live forever with him in heaven someday.**

For our craft, we're going to turn this plain, boring clear sheet into a beautiful window decoration. Show children the sample craft. If you have a window in your room, hold the sample craft up against the glass so children can see the light shine through the colored tissue paper. Say: **Our colorful window decorations can help us remember Jesus' beautiful love for us!**

Have kids begin by gluing the red tissue-paper squares along the outline of the heart. Children can each dip a paintbrush into the watered-down glue, paint the glue along the outline of the heart, and press tissue-paper squares onto the glue. As children work, encourage them to talk about people they love.

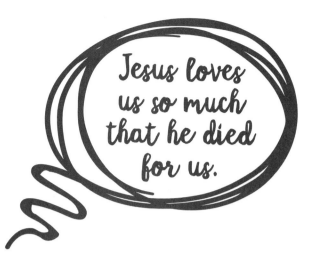

Jesus loves us so much that he died for us.

Once children have finished covering the heart outline in red squares, they can cover the cross in a different color of their choice. Finally, kids can choose a third color to cover the rest of the transparency.

Use a hole punch to make a hole at each of the two top corners of children's transparencies. Help children tie a length of yarn through the two holes so the craft can be hung easily.

If you have access to a window, hold up kids' crafts to the light so they can see what they look like, and remind children they can hang their crafts in a window at home to remember how much Jesus loves them.

TIP!

Ages 6-7
Leave sheets of tissue paper whole for older kids, and let them tear off pieces as they make their craft.

STAINED GLASS WINDOW TEMPLATE

JESUS RISES FROM THE DEAD

Matthew 28:1-10; Mark 16:1-11;
Luke 24:1-12; John 20:1-18

Supplies
- white card stock (½ sheet per child)
- white coffee filters (1 per child)
- gold or silver chenille wires (½ wire per child)
- paper plates (1 per child)
- markers
- washable school glue
- silver or gold glitter
- transparent tape

Easy Prep
- Cut the sheets of card stock in half so that each piece is about 8½x5½ inches.
- Cut the chenille wires in half.
- Make a sample craft to show kids.

ANGEL MEGAPHONES

What Kids Will Do
Kids make angel crafts.

Make an Angel
Say: **After Jesus died, his friends went to the tomb where he was buried. But they were so confused. Jesus' body wasn't there! Where could he be? An angel from heaven was there. The Bible says the angel's face was as bright as lightning and his clothes were as white as snow. Wow! The angel told Jesus' friends, "He isn't here! He is risen from the dead!" Then the angel told Jesus' friends to tell everyone the good news that** <u>Jesus is alive now</u>! Show children the sample craft. **Let's make an angel craft to remember the good news that the angel shared. We can use our craft to share that** <u>Jesus is alive now</u> **with other people, too.** Show children how to use the craft as a megaphone by putting the bottom of the tube up to your lips and shouting, "Jesus is alive now!"

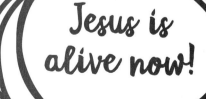

Jesus is alive now!

Give each child a piece of white card stock, and help kids each roll it into a tube and tape the outside edge of the card stock in place. Kids can then use markers to draw a smiley face on one end of the tube.

Next, help children fold a coffee filter in half and tape the coffee filter to the back of the tube to create angel wings.

To create a halo, help children loop one end of a section of chenille wire into a circle and then tape the other end of the wire to the back of the paper tube.

Finally, kids can lay the angel on a paper plate and add thin lines of washable glue to the coffee filter wings and the tube. Once children have created lines of glue, help them gently shake glitter over the glue.

Share the Good News!
Allow the angel megaphones to dry completely; then help children shake off the excess glitter onto the paper plates. Let children use their megaphones to shout that Jesus is alive now!

THE EMPTY TOMB

Luke 23:26–24:12

Supplies

- white paper plates (2 per child)
- crayons
- stapler
- gray, brown, or black tissue paper
- "Jesus Is Alive" handout (1 copy for every 3 kids) (p. 165)

Easy Prep

- Cut a 3-inch hole in the center of 1 plate for each child.
- Cut apart the strips of the "Jesus Is Alive" handout so you have 1 strip per child.
- Make a sample craft to show kids.

JESUS' TOMB

What Kids Will Do
Kids make tombs.

Color the Tomb
Give each child one whole paper plate and one with a hole in it.

Say: **Jesus is our Savior. He died for us and was buried in a tomb. A tomb is kind of like a cave. Color the bottom of both your plates. You might want to color them so they look like rocks.**

Allow time for kids to color their plates. As kids begin to finish coloring, staple their plates together with the tops of the plates facing in. Allow enough space between two staples for the "Jesus Is Alive" strips to fit through.

Say: **Some people put Jesus in the tomb. Let's add Jesus to our tombs.**

Have each child color the Jesus figure on the "Jesus Is Alive" strips. Then help kids slide the strip in between the plates so they can see Jesus through the hole.

Say: **The guards put a huge rock in front of Jesus' tomb. Let's add a rock to our tomb.** Have children crumple tissue paper into large wads that they can stuff into the holes in their plates.

Play Peek-a-Boo
Say: **In three days, Jesus came back to life! His tomb was empty!** Have kids slide "Jesus" out of the way of the hole and then remove the rocks.

Have children use their craft and practice telling the story on their own.

Jesus is our Savior.

Talk About It

Say: <u>Jesus is our Savior.</u> He died for us. But he didn't stay dead! The tomb is empty and Jesus is alive!

Ask:

- Who can you tell that Jesus is alive?

Cheer About It

Lead children in this cheer to celebrate Jesus being alive.

Hip, hip hooray,
Jesus is alive today!
Hip, hip hooray,
Jesus is alive today!

JESUS iS ALiVE

THE ROAD TO EMMAUS

Luke 24:13-35

Supplies

- index cards
- chenille wires (3 per child)
- washable markers
- yarn
- glue sticks
- transparent tape
- glitter glue

Easy Prep

- Cut the index cards in half so that each child will have 3 halves.
- Cut the yarn into short pieces, each about 3 inches long.
- Make a sample craft to show kids.

JESUS & FRIENDS FINGER PUPPETS

What Kids Will Do

Kids make finger puppets.

Make Finger Puppets

Say: **One day, two of Jesus' friends were walking along a road and were very sad because Jesus had died on the cross. They didn't know that Jesus had come back to life! But Jesus showed his friends who he was. Let's make finger puppets of the people in the Bible story.** Show children the sample craft, and point out that two of the finger puppets will represent Jesus' friends and the finger puppet with the glitter on it represents Jesus.

Give each child three index-card pieces, and have kids draw a face on each card with the markers.

Jesus shows us who he is.

After drawing a face on each of their cards, children can glue yarn to the top of the cards as hair for their puppets. Then help kids smear glitter glue on the card they want to be their Jesus puppet.

Finally, help children tape a chenille wire to the back of each card, and show them how to wrap the wire around a finger to create the "body" of the puppet, which will go over a finger.

Act Out the Bible Story

After kids have finished making their puppets, have them put the puppets on their fingers and act out the Bible story as you say the following rhyme.

Jesus' friends went walking by.
They were sad because Jesus died.
But then a stranger to them appeared.
Who was this? It was not clear.
They talked and shared and ate a meal.
It was Jesus—he was real!
Jesus shows us who he is,
He loves us, and we are his!

TIP!

Ages 6-7
Instead of using the rhyme with older kids, have them get into pairs to act out the Bible story. Have kids take turns, with one child being Jesus and the other child being the two disciples.

JESUS APPEARS TO DISCIPLES

Mark 16:14; Luke 24:36-43; John 20:19-31

Supplies

- white construction paper folded in half like a greeting card (2 sheets per child)
- "Pop-Up Jesus Figure" handout (1 copy for every 4 children) (p. 171)
- markers or crayons
- glue sticks
- safety scissors

Easy Prep

- Cut out a Jesus figure from the handout for each child.
- Make a sample craft to show kids.

JESUS POP-UP CARDS

What Kids Will Do

Kids make pop-up cards.

Make Pop-Up Cards

Say: **In this Bible story, Jesus surprised his friends in a big way! Jesus' friends were all together inside a locked room. They made sure no one else would be able to get in. But then suddenly Jesus appeared inside the room and was standing with them! Jesus showed up in a surprising way to help his friends believe in him and know that he really did come back to life. Our craft will help us remember the Bible story.** Show children the sample craft.

Give each child a folded sheet of construction paper, and help kids make two cuts approximately 1-inch long into the center folded part of the paper. The cuts can be about an inch or farther apart, and they don't need to be exactly parallel for the craft to work, so let kids try to make the cuts themselves. Then help children fold the cut section inward to make a small "L" or box shape. This will be the base for the pop-up Jesus figure inside the card (see photo 1 on page 170).

Then give each child a Jesus figure, and help kids glue the back of the Jesus figure to the pop-up base. Next, help children glue the cut sheet of paper with the Jesus figure in it to the inside of a second folded sheet of paper—this way the pop-up cutout area won't be seen from the outside of the card (see photo 2 on page 170).

Once the sheets of paper are glued together, children can draw a house on the front of the card with crayons or markers. Have kids draw a door on the house as well, reminding them that Jesus' friends locked the door to their room in the Bible story. Inside the card, children can draw the inside of the house, adding pictures of Jesus' friends and coloring the Jesus figure (see photo 3 on page 170).

Jesus helps us believe in him.

Talk About It

Say: **We're learning that** <u>Jesus helps us believe in him</u>**. One way** <u>Jesus helps us believe in him</u> **is by giving us people who tell us more about him. And we can do the same thing for others. You can show your card to someone and tell that person how Jesus surprised his friends.** Hold up the sample craft. **Jesus' friends were inside a room together.** Point to the door on the house. **They made sure the door was locked so no one could get in. But all of a sudden, Jesus appeared inside the room with them!** Open up the card to show the pop-up Jesus figure. **Jesus appeared to his friends to show that he came back to life after dying for us. That's how much he loves us. You can remind the people you show your card to that Jesus loves them so much, too!**

POP-UP JESUS FiGURE

JESUS TALKS WITH PETER

John 13:31-38; 18:15-18, 25-27; 21:15-25

Supplies

- "Heart Lacing Template" handout printed on colored card stock (1 copy per child) (p. 175)
- colored plastic lacing (10 feet per child)
- crayons
- duct tape or masking tape
- hole punch
- transparent tape

Easy Prep

- Cut out the heart shapes, and use a hole punch to punch out the black circles around each heart.
- Make a sample craft to show kids.

HEART LACING

What Kids Will Do

Kids make heart-lacing crafts.

Make a Lacing Heart

Show children the sample craft.

Say: **This fun heart craft will remind us that <u>Jesus believes in us</u>!** Show children how they'll lace the plastic string through the holes in the heart.

Give each child a card stock heart, and set out the crayons to share. Tell children not to color over the numbers around the perimeter of the hearts so that they can still see them.

TIP!

Ages 6-7

Let older kids each cut out a heart shape and use a hole punch to punch out the holes around the edge of the heart. Have kids practice using the hole punch on a scrap piece of paper before they use it on the heart.

After they've colored their hearts, help each child tape one end of a 10-foot piece of lacing to the back of the heart.

Once the plastic lacing is attached, children can lace the string through the holes by guiding the end of the string through the numbered holes in order from 1 to 20. If you have younger children in your class, you can encourage them to search for the numbers they know, but they don't have to follow the number order to lace their hearts.

When children have finished lacing, have them unlace the strings and play again. They can lace the strings in reverse order (lacing from number 20 to 1), they can follow the holes around the perimeter of the heart, or they can make up their own lacing pattern.

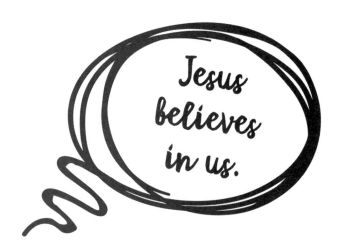

Jesus believes in us.

Say: **Good job, friends! Lacing the string through the holes was kind of hard and took concentration. But <u>Jesus believes in us</u> to do big and hard things. One big thing <u>Jesus believes in you</u> to do is share his love with everyone—even if it seems hard sometimes. You can share Jesus' love by playing with someone who's left out on the playground or by using kind words even if someone says something mean to you. There are so many ways to share Jesus' love. When you take your craft home, the heart shape can remind you to show Jesus' love all the time...even when it feels hard! <u>Jesus believes in you</u> to share his love.**

TIP!

Ages 6-7
After lacing the heart from 1 to 20, encourage older kids to make new designs by lacing their hearts in different ways.

HEART LACING TEMPLATE

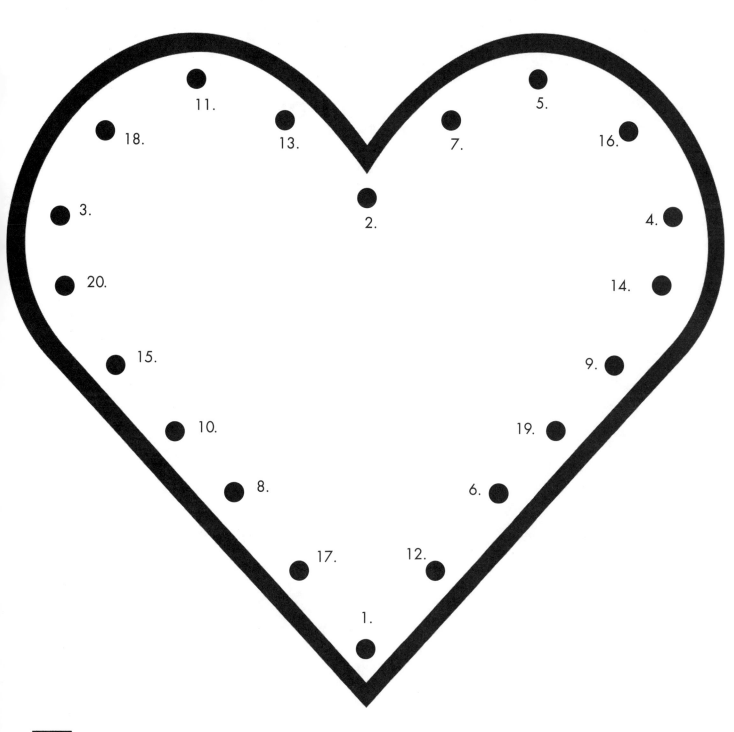

THE GREAT COMMISSION

Matthew 28:16-20; Mark 16:15-20;
Luke 24:44-53; Acts 1:6-11

Supplies

- "Person Shape" handout printed on white card stock (1 copy per child) (p. 179)
- jumbo craft stick (1 per child)
- hair-colored yarn (brown, black, yellow, red)
- crayons
- colored tissue paper
- glue sticks
- transparent tape
- lamp, large flashlight, or overhead projector to make shadows

Easy Prep

- Cut out a person shape for each child.
- Cut the yarn into about 6-inch lengths.
- Cut the tissue paper into approximately 1x1-inch squares.
- Make a sample craft to show kids.

SHADOW PUPPETS

What Kids Will Do
Kids make shadow puppets.

Explore Their Shadows
Say: **Jesus is always with us. Something else that sticks with us all the time are our shadows! Sometimes we can see our shadows really well, like when we're outside on a hot, bright summer day. But other times we might not notice our shadows as much or even realize they're there.**

Turn on a lamp, flashlight, or overhead projector, and shine the light toward a wall. Then turn off the main lights in your room, and invite children to stand between the light and the wall and make silly shadows with their hands, arms, and/or bodies.

After a minute or so, turn the main room lights back on.

TIP!

Ages 6-7
Let older kids cut out the person shape from the card stock and the tissue paper squares.

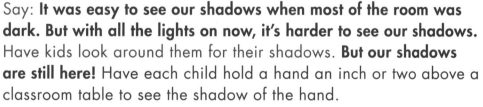

Say: **It was easy to see our shadows when most of the room was dark. But with all the lights on now, it's harder to see our shadows.** Have kids look around them for their shadows. **But our shadows are still here!** Have each child hold a hand an inch or two above a classroom table to see the shadow of the hand.

Say: **Just like we can know that our shadows are with us even though we don't notice them sometimes, we can know that <u>Jesus is always with us</u>! Jesus is quietly beside us *all* the time, whether we realize it or not. We can't see Jesus with our eyes, but we can feel and know that <u>Jesus is always with us</u>. We're going to make shadow puppets to remember that <u>Jesus is always with us</u>, like our shadows!** Show children the sample craft.

Jesus is always with us.

Make Puppets

Give each child a person-shaped piece of card stock. Have children decorate their paper-people to look like them. They can draw faces on their people with crayons and glue on yarn hair that matches their hair color.

Then children can glue tissue-paper squares to their people to look like clothes.

Once kids have finished decorating their paper people, have them turn the shapes over, and help each child tape a jumbo craft stick to the bottom of one of the legs to make the puppet handle.

Play With Shadow Puppets

When children have finished making their puppets, turn the lamp or flashlight back on and the overhead lights off, and let kids play with their shadow puppets against the lit wall.

Say: **When you play with your shadow puppet at home or even when you see your own shadow, you can remember that <u>Jesus is always with you</u>, just like your shadow!**

PERSON SHAPE

OK
TO COPY

Scripture Index

Matthew

An Angel Announces Jesus' Birth
(Matthew 1:18-25) 8-9
Wise Men Worship King Jesus
(Matthew 2:1-18) 18-19
John Baptizes Jesus
(Matthew 3)...22-25
Satan Tempts Jesus
(Matthew 4:1-11) 26-31
Wise and Foolish Builder
(Matthew 7:24-27) 58-59
Jesus Eats With Sinners at Matthew's House
(Matthew 9:9-13) 60-63
A Roman Officer Demonstrates Faith
(Matthew 8:5-13) 68-71
Jesus Eases John's Doubt
(Matthew 11:1-6) 72-73
Parable of the Farmer and the Seed
(Matthew 13:1-9, 18-23)......................74-75
Jesus Describes His True Family
(Matthew 12:46-50) 76-77
Jesus Calms the Storm
(Matthew 8:23-27) 78-79
Jesus Heals a Bleeding Woman and
Restores a Girl to Life
(Matthew 9:18-26) 80-83
Jesus Walks on Water
(Matthew 14:22-33) 84-87
Jesus Is Transfigured
(Matthew 17:1-13) 88-91
Jesus Feeds Five Thousand
(Matthew 14:13-21) 96-97
Disciples Argue About Who Will Be the Greatest
(Matthew 18:1-6) 98-101
Jesus Blesses the Children
(Matthew 19:13-15) 132-133
Jesus Heals Blind Men
(Matthew 20:29-34) 134-135
Jesus' Triumphant Entry
(Matthew 21:1-11) 140-143
The Plot to Kill Jesus
(Matthew 26:1-5, 14-16)................... 146-149
Jesus Is Betrayed and Arrested
(Matthew 26:47-56) 152-153
Jesus Is Put on Trial
(Matthew 27:15-31) 154-155
Jesus Is Crucified
(Matthew 27:32-61) 156-159
Jesus Rises From the Dead
(Matthew 28:1-10) 160-161
The Great Commission
(Matthew 28:16-20) 176-179

Mark

Satan Tempts Jesus
(Mark 1:12-13) 26-31
Jesus Calls Disciples
(Mark 1:16-20) 32-37
Jesus Describes His True Family
(Mark 3:31-35) 76-77
Jesus Calms the Storm
(Mark 4:35-41) 78-79
Jesus Heals a Bleeding Woman and
Restores a Girl to Life
(Mark 5:21-43) 80-83
Jesus Walks on Water
(Mark 6:45-52) 84-87
Jesus Is Transfigured
(Mark 9:2-13) 88-91
Jesus Feeds Five Thousand
(Mark 6:30-44) 96-97
Disciples Argue About Who Will Be the Greatest
(Mark 9:33-37) 98-101
Jesus Blesses the Children
(Mark 10:13-16) 132-133
Jesus Heals Blind Men
(Mark 10:46-52) 134-135
Jesus' Triumphant Entry
(Mark 11:1-11) 140-143
The Poor Widow's Offering
(Mark 12:41-44) 144-145
The Plot to Kill Jesus
(Mark 14:1-2, 10-11).. 146-149
Jesus Is Betrayed and Arrested
(Mark 14:43-52) 152-153
Jesus Is Put on Trial
(Mark 15:6-15) 154-155
Jesus Is Crucified
(Mark 15:21-47) 156-159
Jesus Rises From the Dead
(Mark 16:1-11) 160-161
Jesus Appears to Disciples
(Mark 16:14)................................... 168-171
The Great Commission
(Mark 16:15-20) 176-179

Luke

An Angel Announces Jesus' Birth
(Luke 1:26-38) 8-9
The First Christmas
(Luke 2:1-7) 10-13
Jesus, the Light of the World, Is Born
(Luke 2:1-20) 14-15
Simeon and Anna See Jesus
(Luke 2:21-40) 16-17
Jesus Speaks With the Religious Teachers
(Luke 2:41-52) 20-21
John Baptizes Jesus
(Luke 3:21-22) 22-25

Satan Tempts Jesus
    (Luke 4:1-13) 26-31
Jesus Is Rejected
    (Luke 4:16-30) 44-47
Jesus Heals People
    (Luke 4:38-40; 5:12-16) 48-51
Jesus Forgives a Paralyzed Man
    (Luke 5:17-26) 52-53
A Miraculous Catch of Fish
    (Luke 5:1-11) 54-57
A Roman Officer Demonstrates Faith
    (Luke 7:1-10) 68-71
Jesus Eases John's Doubt
    (Luke 7:18-23) 72-73
Parable of the Farmer and the Seed
    (Luke 8:4-15) 74-75
Jesus Describes His True Family
    (Luke 8:19-21) 76-77
Jesus Calms the Storm
    (Luke 8:22-25) 78-79
Jesus Heals a Bleeding Woman and
  Restores a Girl to Life
    (Luke 8:40-56) 80-83
Jesus Is Transfigured
    (Luke 9:28-36) 88-91
Parable of the Good Samaritan
    (Luke 10:25-37) 92-95
Jesus Feeds Five Thousand
    (Luke 9:10-17) 96-97
Disciples Argue About Who Will Be the Greatest
    (Luke 9:46-48) 98-101
Jesus Visits Mary and Martha
    (Luke 10:38-42) 106-107
Jesus Heals a Crippled Woman
    (Luke 13:10-17) 108-111
Parables of the Lost Sheep and Lost Coin
    (Luke 15:1-10) 118-121
Parable of the Prodigal Son
    (Luke 15:11-32) 122-125
Jesus Heals Ten Men of Leprosy
    (Luke 17:11-19) 130-131
Jesus Blesses the Children
    (Luke 18:15-17) 132-133
Jesus Heals Blind Men
    (Luke 18:35-43) 134-135
Jesus Meets Zacchaeus
    (Luke 19:1-10) 136-139
Jesus' Triumphant Entry
    (Luke 19:28-40) 140-143
The Poor Widow's Offering
    (Luke 21:1-4) 144-145
The Plot to Kill Jesus
    (Luke 22:1-6) 146-149
Jesus Is Betrayed and Arrested
    (Luke 22:47-53) 152-153

Jesus Is Put on Trial
    (Luke 23:1-25) 154-155
Jesus Is Crucified
    (Luke 23:26-56) 156-159
Jesus Rises From the Dead
    (Luke 24:1-12) 160-161
The Empty Tomb
    (Luke 23:26–24:12) 162-165
The Road to Emmaus
    (Luke 24:13-35) 166-167
Jesus Appears to Disciples
    (Luke 24:36-43) 168-171
The Great Commission
    (Luke 24:44-53) 176-179

John
Jesus Calls Disciples
    (John 1:35-51) 32-37
Jesus Performs His First Miracle
    (John 2:1-12) 38-41
Nicodemus Visits Jesus at Night
    (John 3:1-21) 42-43
Jesus Heals a Lame Man by a Pool
    (John 5:1-18) 64-67
Jesus Walks on Water
    (John 6:16-21) 84-87
Jesus Feeds Five Thousand
    (John 6:1-15) 96-97
Jesus Forgives a Woman
    (John 8:1-11) 102-105
Jesus Heals a Blind Man
    (John 9:1-41) 112-115
Jesus Claims to Be God's Son
    (John 10:22-42) 116-117
Jesus Raises Lazarus From the Dead
    (John 11:1-44) 126-129
Jesus' Triumphant Entry
    (John 12:12-16) 140-143
Jesus Washes His Disciples' Feet
    (John 13:1-17) 150-151
Jesus Is Betrayed and Arrested
    (John 18:1-11) 152-153
Jesus Is Put on Trial
    (John 18:28–19:16) 154-155
Jesus Is Crucified
    (John 19:17-42) 156-159
Jesus Rises From the Dead
    (John 20:1-18) 160-161
Jesus Appears to Disciples
    (John 20:19-31) 168-171
Jesus Talks With Peter
    (John 13:31-38; 18:15-18, 25-27; 21:15-25)
   172-175

Acts
The Great Commission
    (Acts 1:6-11) 176-179

Topical Index

Change

Jesus Calls Disciples (Mark 1:16-20; John 1:35-51)
Jesus can change our lives. 32-37

Jesus Meets Zacchaeus (Luke 19:1-10)
When we spend time with Jesus, he changes us ...
.... 136-139

Children

Jesus Blesses the Children (Matthew 19:13-15;
Mark 10:13-16; Luke 18:15-17)
Jesus wants to be with children. 132-133

Choices

Satan Tempts Jesus (Matthew 4:1-11; Mark 1:12-13;
Luke 4:1-13)
Jesus shows us the right way. 26-31

Jesus Heals a Crippled Woman (Luke 13:10-17)
Jesus does what's right—no matter what ... 108-111

Christmas

The First Christmas (Luke 2:1-7)
Jesus is the best gift ever. 10-13

Jesus, the Light of the World, Is Born (Luke 2:1-20)
Jesus is the light of the world. 14-15

Simeon and Anna See Jesus (Luke 2:21-40)
Jesus is God's gift... 16-17

Wise Men Worship King Jesus (Matthew 2:1-18)
Jesus is the King. 18-19

Easter

Jesus Is Put on Trial (Matthew 27:15-31; Mark 15:6-
15; Luke 23:1-25; John 18:28–19:16)
Jesus understands suffering. 154-155

Jesus Is Crucified (Matthew 27:32-61; Mark 15:21-
47; Luke 23:26-56; John 19:17-42)
Jesus loves us so much that he died for us ....
.... 156-159

Jesus Rises From the Dead (Matthew 28:1-10;
Mark 16:1-11; Luke 24:1-12; John 20:1-18)
Jesus is alive now!.. 160-161

The Empty Tomb (Luke 23:26–24:12)
Jesus is our Savior............................. 162-165

Jesus Appears to Disciples (Mark 16:14;
Luke 24:36-43; John 20:19-31)
Jesus helps us believe in him.............. 168-171

Empowerment

Jesus Talks With Peter (John 13:31-38; 18:15-18,
25-27; 21:15-25)
Jesus believes in us............................ 172-175

The Great Commission (Matthew 28:16-20;
Mark 16:15-20; Luke 24:44-53; Acts 1:6-11)
Jesus is always with us....................... 176-179

Eternal Life

Nicodemus Visits Jesus at Night (John 3:1-21)
Jesus gives us eternal life........................42-43

Family

Jesus Describes His True Family (Matthew 12:46-50;
Mark 3:31-35; Luke 8:19-21)
Jesus wants us in his family.....................76-77

Fear

Jesus Walks on Water (Matthew 14:22-33;
Mark 6:45-52; John 6:16-21)
Jesus calms our fears.. 84-87

Forgiveness

Jesus Forgives a Paralyzed Man (Luke 5:17-26)
Jesus forgives us.....................................52-53

Jesus Forgives a Woman (John 8:1-11)
Jesus forgives...................................... 102-105

Friendship

Jesus Visits Mary and Martha (Luke 10:38-42)
Jesus wants to be our friend................ 106-107

The Plot to Kill Jesus (Luke 22:1-6; Matthew 26:1-5,
14-16; Mark 14:1-2, 10-11)
Jesus knows what it's like to be hurt by a friend....
.... 146-149

Giving

The Poor Widow's Offering (Mark 12:41-44;
Luke 21:1-4)
Jesus loves givers.............................. 144-145

Healing

Jesus Heals People (Luke 4:38-40; 5:12-16)
Jesus heals us...48-51

Jesus Heals a Bleeding Woman and Restores a Girl to Life
(Matthew 9:18-26; Mark 5:21-43; Luke 8:40-56)
Jesus has power over sickness and death 80-83

Humility

Disciples Argue About Who Will Be the Greatest
(Matthew 18:1-6; Mark 9:33-37; Luke 9:46-48)
Jesus shows us what it means to be great.... 98-101

Impossible

An Angel Announces Jesus' Birth (Luke 1:26-38;
Matthew 1:18-25)
God does the impossible............................8-9

Jesus' Identity

John Baptizes Jesus (Matthew 3; Luke 3:21-22)
Jesus is God's Son. 22-25
Jesus Heals a Lame Man by a Pool (John 5:1-18)
Jesus is God...64-67
Jesus Eases John's Doubt (Matthew 11:1-6;
Luke 7:18-23)
Jesus is the Messiah. 72-73
Jesus Is Transfigured (Matthew 17:1-13;
Mark 9:2-13; Luke 9:28-36)
Jesus is God...88-91
Jesus Claims to Be God's Son (John 10:22-42)
Jesus is God's Son. 116-117
Jesus' Triumphant Entry (Matthew 21:1-11;
Mark 11:1-11; Luke 19:28-40; John 12:12-16)
Jesus is the King...... 140-143
The Road to Emmaus (Luke 24:13-35)
Jesus shows us who he is 166-167

Love

Jesus Is Rejected (Luke 4:16-30)
Jesus loves everyone 44-47
Jesus Eats With Sinners at Matthew's House
(Matthew 9:9-13)
Jesus came for everyone.. 60-63
Parable of the Good Samaritan (Luke 10:25-37)
Jesus-followers care for others.................92-95
Parables of the Lost Sheep and Lost Coin
(Luke 15:1-10)
Jesus looks for us.... 118-121
Parable of the Prodigal Son (Luke 15:11-32)
Jesus loves us no matter what. 122-125
Jesus Is Betrayed and Arrested (Matthew 26:47-56;
Mark 14:43-52; Luke 22:47-53; John 18:1-11)
Jesus loves even his enemies..............152-153

Power

Jesus Performs His First Miracle (John 2:1-12)
Jesus has God's power. 38-41
A Miraculous Catch of Fish (Luke 5:1-11)
Jesus is amazing....................................54-57
A Roman Officer Demonstrates Faith (Luke 7:1-10;
Matthew 8:5-13)
Jesus has authority over everything..........68-71
Jesus Calms the Storm (Matthew 8:23-27;
Mark 4:35-41; Luke 8:22-25)
Jesus has power to calm storms...............78-79
Jesus Heals a Bleeding Woman and Restores a Girl to Life
(Mark 5:21-43; Matthew 9:18-26; Luke 8:40-56)
Jesus has power over sickness and death....80-83
Jesus Feeds Five Thousand (Matthew 14:13-21;
Mark 6:30-44; Luke 9:10-17; John 6:1-15)
Jesus does the unexpected......................96-97
Jesus Heals a Blind Man (John 9:1-41)
Jesus has the power to heal................112-115
Jesus Raises Lazarus From the Dead (John 11:1-44)
Jesus has power over death................126-129

Prayer

Jesus Heals Blind Men (Matthew 20:29-34;
Mark 10:46-52; Luke 18:35-43)
Jesus hears us...................................134-135

Serving

Jesus Washes His Disciples' Feet (John 13:1-17)
Jesus shows us how to serve. 150-151

Spiritual Growth

Parable of the Farmer and the Seed (Matthew
13:1-9, 18-23; Luke 8:4-15)
Jesus grows us.....................................74-75

Thankfulness

Jesus Heals Ten Men of Leprosy (Luke 17:11-19)
Jesus deserves our thanks...................130-131

Wisdom

Jesus Speaks With the Religious Teachers
(Luke 2:41-52)
Jesus is wise..20-21
Wise and Foolish Builder (Matthew 7:24-27)
Jesus is trustworthy...............................58-59